Also by Constance Bovier

Non-Fiction

More God
From the Twelve Steps into Deeper Faith

From the Crucible
When Recovery and Religion Merge

Fiction

Restoring Hope
A Collection of Stories

Dream Animal Wisdom

Practical and Profound Guidance from Our Nighttime Visitors

Constance Bovier

BALBOA.PRESS
A DIVISION OF HAY HOUSE

Copyright © 2021 Constance Bovier.

All rights reserved. No part of this book may be used or reproduced by any means, graphic, electronic, or mechanical, including photocopying, recording, taping or by any information storage retrieval system without the written permission of the author except in the case of brief quotations embodied in critical articles and reviews.

Scripture quotations marked NIV are taken from the Holy Bible, New International Version®. NIV®. Copyright © 1973, 1978, 1984 by International Bible Society. Used by permission of Zondervan. All rights reserved. [Biblica]

Balboa Press books may be ordered through booksellers or by contacting:

Balboa Press
A Division of Hay House
1663 Liberty Drive
Bloomington, IN 47403
www.balboapress.com
844-682-1282

Because of the dynamic nature of the Internet, any web addresses or links contained in this book may have changed since publication and may no longer be valid. The views expressed in this work are solely those of the author and do not necessarily reflect the views of the publisher, and the publisher hereby disclaims any responsibility for them.

The author of this book does not dispense medical advice or prescribe the use of any technique as a form of treatment for physical, emotional, or medical problems without the advice of a physician, either directly or indirectly. The intent of the author is only to offer information of a general nature to help you in your quest for emotional and spiritual well-being. In the event you use any of the information in this book for yourself, which is your constitutional right, the author and the publisher assume no responsibility for your actions.

Author Photo Credit: Peter Wolfe

Print information available on the last page.

ISBN: 978-1-9822-6371-3 (sc)
ISBN: 978-1-9822-6372-0 (e)

Balboa Press rev. date: 02/25/2021

Permission to use all included dreams includes first-time rights only. Dreamers retain the right to use their dreams in whatever way they wish in the future. Dreamers have chosen the names by which they prefer to be identified in this work.

Epigraph for *Community Connections* chapter: Excerpted from the book *The Emotional Lives of Animals*, p. 30-31. Copyright © 2007 by Marc Bekoff. Reprinted with permission from New World Library. www.NewWorldLibrary.com

Epigraphs by Robert J. Hoss are reprinted by his permission, excerpted from the book *Dream Language: A Handbook for Dreamwork*, 2nd Edition, PDF Version. www.dreamscience.org

Cover Art:
PEACEABLE KINGDOM
Copyright 1994 by John August Swanson
Serigraph, 30" x 22½"
www.JohnAugustSwanson.com

For my dear husband Peter Wolfe,
unfailing encourager and supporter of all my dreams,
both waking and sleeping.

Dreamed the night before the inaugural
meeting of my dream group in 2009:

Dangerous Dreamers

I am driving slowly down a long, two-lane road bordered by woods. Many cars are on the road with me. The going is slow because people keep stopping to let their dogs out of their cars to run around in the road. Then a man driving toward me on the wrong side of the road stops and lets two bears out of his car. I'm apprehensive about all these drivers and their animals.

Warning: Unpredictability ahead!

CONTENTS

Preface xiii
Introduction – A Journey at the Heart Level xvii

Part I - Creatures in the Spotlight 1

    Dogs: Leashes and Loyalty 3
    Horses: Nobility and Resilience 11
    Cats: Creatures of My Heart 21
    Cats: The Wild Ones 31
    Birds: On the Wing 43
    Snakes: Primitive Power 55
    Sea Creatures: Deep Calls to Deep 67
    Bugs: The Many-Legged 81
    Turtles: Ancient Ones 93

Interlude – A Visitation 109

Part II - Focus on Themes 113

    Spiritual Menagerie 115
    Diamonds in the Details 127
    Who's in Charge Here? 143
    Composite Creatures 153
    MoleCat's Revelation 163
    Life, Death and Resurrection 173
    Transformations 183
    Ancestral Callings 193
    Community Connections 201
    The Promise of More to Come 217

Notes 225

Appendices
    I – Glossary 235
    II – Reading Recommendations 239
    III – Ways to Engage Our Dream Animals.........................243
    IV – Guided Meditation with a Dream Animal...................249

Acknowledgments..251
About the Author..253

PREFACE

In my mind, I can still slip back into my front-row chair in a spartan church classroom, on a blustery fall Saturday in 2003. Surrounded by my classmates in spiritual director training, I listened to a wise and funny Episcopal priest's spellbinding presentation about dreamwork. Dreams had made little impression upon my life before then ... well, except for that one little recurring childhood nightmare. But on that day, something buried within me snapped to attention and responded with a resounding *YES*! In an instant, I intuitively knew that dreamwork was destined to become a core spiritual practice for me – as essential and as integral as prayer.

This is exactly what has happened.

At the time of my spiritual director training, I'd been living the Twelve-Step recovery program for more than 20 years. Those familiar with the Twelve Steps know that a rigorous commitment to that process can lead to dramatic emotional and spiritual transformations, and I'm sure I was a bit complacent, maybe even a bit arrogant, about the level of self-awareness and personal growth I'd already achieved.

Dreamwork was about to thrust me into a realm of self-discovery that I hadn't known existed.

My new commitment to dream-tending burst open the channel from the unconscious, which had been trembling for years with pent-up truths. With my newly awakened recall, the Dream Maker began delivering up images like a spongy layer of grass in my backyard where I feared someone might step, plunging into the ominous chasm I knew lay below. Frustratingly the new dimensions of awareness arrived enveloped in metaphor. What does *this* mean? What kind of weird dream is *that*? But I persisted, motivated by the conviction that every minute spent journaling and reflecting upon my dreams would be worth it – somehow, sometime, in some mysterious way.

Soon I found myself sharing my nocturnal adventures with a variety of creatures. I knew that my dream animals were bringing messages, which I couldn't begin to decipher on my own. Working solo in my early days, I turned too quickly to dream symbol books – something I adamantly discourage today as the starting point for anyone. While I found some dream animal interpretations interesting, much of the material I read was far off the mark for what I sensed was true about my own dream creatures. Even learning that animals typically represent our deep instincts or energies wasn't particularly useful. How was that supposed to help me in my waking life?

Being a perpetual student, I dove into the writings of dreamwork pioneers like Morton Kelsey, John Sanford, Robert Johnson, Jeremy Taylor, and began exploring the foundational wisdom of Carl Jung. I attended workshops and conferences brimming over with rich material about the relationship of dreams to myth, religion and fairy tales. While I learned that many of my dream images like a square spiderweb, a two-headed frog and a mothering snake have their roots in archetype, I longed for something less lofty psychologically and academically, a more down-to-earth entryway to working with my dream animals.

How could I, an ordinary dreamer well-grounded in my faith tradition, more fully engage my dream creatures and their energies? How might I invite a dream creature to help illuminate my way of being in the world, of relating to myself, to others and to the divine? Most importantly, how might these internal energies in animal garb encourage me forward on my journey of individuation, of becoming the person I was created to be?

This book is my attempt to address these questions. It is the resource I wish had been available to me when I first began dreamwork.

In this compilation of animal dreams, I seek to demonstrate a variety of ways that a dreamer may welcome and embrace the creatures within. The book is divided into two sections: Part I offers chapters focused on some of the most common dream creatures; Part II explores in greater depth a variety of topics and themes that

I believe warrant close attention and shows how a variety of dream creatures help to convey those themes.

The dreamers who've joined me in this endeavor range from new dreamworkers to those who've been dream-tending for decades. The result is a broad spectrum of dream processing – from the straightforward, beginning level, to the deeply profound. Interpretations, which always emphasize the dreamer's personal associations, include insights from research and archetypal studies when those additional levels of meaning emerge organically and in due time through the dreamer's own experience and development.

A supremely invitational truth about dreamwork: we can begin at any time, right where we are. I hope that this book will serve both as a primer for the curious and inspiration for experienced dreamtenders who may never have paused to fully engage the animals who claim them as they sleep.

Whether you read the book chronologically or use it as a reference, may what follows meet you at levels from the ordinary to the marvelous.

May the dear creatures who've gathered here along with their dreamers beckon us all further into the truths of our own deepest selves.

Constance Bovier

Special notes to readers:

- *Grammarians may wonder at verb tenses slithering between past and present. This is deliberate to retain as much immediacy as possible for the dreams themselves and the dreamer's initial processing.*
- *All dreams without attribution are my own.*

INTRODUCTION
A Journey at the Heart Level

*All the creatures I've known ... have been good creatures.
Each individual is a marvel and perfect in his or her own way.
Just being with any animal is edifying, for each has a knowing that
surpasses human understanding .... Knowing someone who belongs
to another species can enlarge your soul in surprising ways.*

Sy Montgomery

I awaken with vibrant energy the morning after returning home from a week-long dream conference. I hurry downstairs for coffee and a protein bar, then trot down another staircase into my dungeon. My fond name for my office acknowledges its place at the lowest level of our townhome – appropriate for one on the Jungian path of individuation – and also its proclivity toward cold in the winter.

Happily, my office has a beautiful view. Beyond the rolling green of a communal backyard, lay the morning-placid waters of Clear Lake with sun-glinted pastel buildings lining the distant shore. This morning my gaze settles on my computer's desktop photo of my daughter cradling a four-pound premature baby goat against her chest. This infant, Charlie, rests his trusting little brown and white head against Kelly's shoulder, eyes closed, peaceful, at one with a human presence. This baby goat needed a great deal of human aid to survive at this point in his fragile little life.

Charlie was part of a little goat herd, the sole survivor of a difficult four-kid pregnancy, requiring round-the-clock bottle-feeding. Visiting the farm, Kelly shared this precious time and I, from afar, experienced Charlie vicariously through texted photos and videos. My delight at each new Charlie sighting hardly surprised me, being part of a family of animal lovers. But I was puzzled by my palpable desire to clasp this little creature to my own heart ... until

I understood that newborn Charlie was part of my grieving for my older sister Carol, who had died only a few months before after living a rural life surrounded by animals.

Sitting at my desk that post-conference morning, I gaze once more at the photo of infant Charlie with my daughter, the adult expression of that which began as a tiny bundle of cells within my own body. In my imagination I press little Charlie against my own heart once again, knowing to my deepest core, for a few time-stilling moments, what it means to be connected in love to all of God's creation.

Then I open a new file in my computer and type the first words of this book.

One of my life's greatest spiritual ironies is that my call to respond to the feral cats at our local park triggered the collapse of my nourishing morning practice of centering prayer. It's tough to sit in silent meditation when you know you need to be out by first light with the humane trap and other accouterments (including enticingly smelly mackerel) in hopes of capturing another elusive community cat for a trip to the local veterinary clinic. The Trap-Neuter-Return program[1] is not for the faint of heart or the slug-a-bed.

Well, one thing led to another. With only one aging cat at home, my husband and I adopted three of the feral kittens from the park. As we socialized and loved those three little packages of life, I continued tending their mama and sister and the other cats who migrated to the little colony in the park. I bestowed benign names like MomCat and KidCat, hoping to discourage my emotional attachment. (You can imagine how well that worked.) After a short time, there was no denying that my concern and care would continue indefinitely.

Our original feeding routine was awkward, to say the least. The cats' primary shelter was a concrete drainage tunnel surrounded by bushes and trees and when heavy Houston rains lashed the area, I had no protected spot for their food dishes. So I decided to create a new feeding station for them on a concrete slope under the bridge bordering the park. A wood-working friend built two L-shaped plywood platforms to create flat surfaces for their bowls and, for several days, I showed the cats their breakfast and led them along the path to their new dining room.

Before long the cats were waiting for me each morning at the new feeding station and our inter-species dynamics changed dramatically. I no longer towered over them and with new proximity came a new perspective. The cats now looked into my eyes and I into theirs. Now we were meeting at the heart level.

Mystified by the strong hold of these feral cats upon my spirit, I took this question to my spiritual director. She listened respectfully, yet I could tell she wasn't as keen on animals as I, and I sometimes suspected that she hoped I would move on to more important things – like why my prayer life had fallen apart. As life would have it, after her retirement, I happened upon a new spiritual director whose love for animals has helped me recognize that my work with the community cats *is* part of my prayer life, that the park is my mission field, and that these cats are an invitation from God to get in touch with my wild, feral self.

And I have come to understand that all the cats in my waking life are communing in a mysterious way with the cat energy that infuses the sacred landscape of my dreams.

Sy Montgomery, quoted in the epigraph above, was asked in an interview what her years as a student of animals had taught her about her life. Her answer: "How to be a good creature."[2] I envision my own individuation as increasing awareness of my place on our planet and in our universe, with diminishing emphasis on humans at the apex of creation with animals on all the lower rungs, simply because they can't speak for themselves.

Throughout the development of this book, I've been wonderfully enriched by the work of contemporary scientists and science writers who unwrap for the rest of us the secrets of consciousness, emotions and intelligence in animals. Fortunately, we've come a long way from the sixties when Jane Goodall was castigated by the scientific establishment for naming and ascribing emotions to her chimpanzees, when animal behaviorists banned whatever was deemed anthropomorphic, helping to perpetuate anthropocentrism, the sense that everything revolves around us.³ Today anyone who watches television or views animal videos online can, for example, affirm the tender mothering of elephants, their bonds of friendship, their grief at the death of a herd member to poaching. Paradoxically our increased sensitivity has swung to the contemporary extreme of wildlife tourism – which is seldom to the benefit of the creatures we admire⁴.

I wonder if our dream creatures might help us find a compassionate stance between brutal (and greedy) exploitation on one hand and romantic (or oblivious) idealization on the other. Might our encounters with flesh and blood creatures in every environment, including our own homes, help us be more accepting and attentive to the animals who enter our lives through our dreams? And the opposite? And what can our dream animals teach us about ourselves?

Just as I want to know more about a dream creature's essence, I believe that at least some of my dream creatures are coming to tell me of my own and to help me draw closer to my true Self, the part of me that recognizes our common genesis and deep relationship.

It seems to me a pure and noble aspiration – to be a good creature. I believe this may be the ultimate heart level, and my dream animals are helping to show me the way.

I see you.
Welcome!
I can almost feel your heartbeat.
I will watch and listen.
I long to know you better.
I know we are kin.

PART I

Creatures in the Spotlight

*Jung considered animals to be our connection with our natural roots
and he described how the animal motif represents
our deeper primitive instinctual nature.
Our personal associations with (or reactions to)
the animals that we see in our dreams
can define what they represent. Sometimes the animal
represents the element they live in....
Sometimes animals may be associated with our deepest instincts or fears.*

Robert Hoss

One of the seminal dream psychologists, Robert L. Van de Castle, published an encyclopedic work, *Our Dreaming Mind*[1], in which he described his research with 4,000 college students. Working with equal numbers of dreams from men and women, he discovered that 7.5 percent contained at least one animal figure, and the seven most common dream animals in order of frequency were dogs, horses, cats, birds, snakes, fish and insects.

Just as Van de Castle's information predicted, my call for animal dreams produced submissions that fell primarily into those same categories. Knowing that the initial curiosity of some readers will be directed to certain animals, I've clustered many dreams into species-specific chapters, following the order of Van de Castle's most common creatures with a few modifications. You will find two chapters devoted to felines – first, the domestic cat; second, the big wild cats. I take some liberties with the fish and insect categories and I include a chapter dedicated to the turtle, which has emerged as a major guide (besides the cat) on my personal dream journey.

At first reading, some dreams may seem deceptively simple, others decidedly complex. In some cases, the dream animal is familiar in general (the species) or in particular (a beloved pet). In other examples, the dreamer is initially confounded by the creature who appears. In every case, the dream animal is uniquely personal to the dreamer, and this is what the processing will illuminate.

I have deliberately chosen to omit summaries of common symbolic meanings for featured animals; a great many books already exist on that subject. Because dreamers, at some level, always know the truth of their own dreams, I allow them to express what their creatures mean to them. Contributors have been warmly willing to probe and ponder their dream materials, and I've plied them with further prompts to encourage processing. Then I've listened as they shared what they intuitively understand their creatures' wisdom is making known.

This is, after all, the central purpose for this book: I believe that dreamwork begins most authentically not with a heady intellectual approach, but at the heart level where the creature engages the dreamer. Therefore, no matter how clearly you or I may see something else in a dream, what's on the page is the dreamer's truth. And most dreamworkers, *including me*, recognize that more is likely to emerge from our most memorable dreams over time.

Throughout this book, you will see dreamers engage their creatures in a variety of ways – as pure instinct or energy, as fragments of self, as unconscious shadow material, as totems, as spirit animal guides, as archetypes or any combination thereof. These terms are individual preferences. We will also see how one's understanding of a creature may deepen and evolve, especially in a dream series. The words a dreamer uses in dream reports and processing can be telling. For instance, "*a* turtle" or "*the* turtle" may become the unadorned noun, "turtle" or ultimately "Turtle", denoting the dreamer's growing awareness of the creature's essence and presence.

So let's begin with a look at the most common of all dream animals, the incomparably relational, loving domestic companion, the dog.

Dogs: Leashes and Loyalty

For more than 12,000 years the dog has lived with
humans as a hunting companion,
protector, object of scorn or adoration and
friend. A subspecies of the gray wolf,
the dog has evolved into more than 400 distinct breeds,
through rudimentary genetic engineering,
to accentuate and enhance specific attributes and
characteristics desired by humans.

Britannica

In casual conversation at a dream conference, a new acquaintance referenced her numerous dog dreams, saying that they were usually her own pets, so she typically dismissed her dog dreams as pleasant and not worth much time or investigation. She went on to describe one perplexing dream that featured her newly acquired rescue dog. "It's a nice enough dog," she said, frowning, "but for some reason, I've not been able to bond with it." She looked startled by her own words. "Oh!" she exclaimed, "I think I have some work to do with that dream!" We smiled at each other and she went away to spend some time with her not-yet-integrated newly rescued energy ... and perhaps with her waking life rescue dog as well.

In reading Virginia Morell's wonderfully warm book, *Animal Wise*[1], I was intrigued by her discussion of how dogs have become so different from wolves through some 50,000 years of domestication. Dogs are so changed that weaned puppies in a lab environment will often choose a human over another dog – definitely *not* the case with hand-raised wolf pups. With this long sharing of our lives – around our campfires, on our hunts, in our homes, it's no wonder the dog carries such familiar energy when it emerges in our dreams.

While dogs may play a spectrum of dream roles, even simple appearances offer us information – new ways to view our current lives and even new directions. Consider the following dream offered by a clergywoman friend with whom I've served in the spiritual direction community:

Off-Leash Dogs
Glynden Bode

On my morning walk, I pass an intersection in my subdivision when I see two BIG dogs, not on leashes. As the dogs begin to run toward me, the owner, a man who is nearly a block away, shouts something at them, which they ignore.

The dogs are tall and slender – their heads near my waist. The first one runs toward me and comes up on my right side, looks me in the eye and licks my hand. The other dog runs very fast to catch up – kind of like a superhero. It looks at me and smiles. Then both dogs turn away, look at me again and trot back towards their owner.

While this dream might have become a nightmare, it contains its own embedded solution. Instead of fleeing in fear or preparing to fend off an anticipated attack, Glynden stands still and watchful as these two sizable dogs race toward her. "Here we are!" they seem to announce as they run to make a connection. By remaining in place, Glynden can receive the gifts of their energies (eye contact, a doggie kiss on her hand and a doggie smile). Notice that these dogs are owned, though not fully controlled, by her masculine self. (We'll have more to say about ownership and gender in the chapter *Who's in Charge Here?*)

Meeting Glynden at an intersection in her life, it seems these deep instincts have come to rescue her (the superhero dog) and to confirm her choice about a waking life dilemma. She receives divine acknowledgment (eye contact) and anointing for her work and ministry (the lick on her hand). After this intentional contact, the dogs leave, looking back, inviting her to come along in their direction, to claim their energy as well as her masculine energy – reemphasizing that she is ready for this integration.

Another spiritual director, dreamworker friend had the following two dog dreams shortly after her retirement when she was feeling "somewhat irrelevant and lost." Her dreams imparted deeply relevant commentary on her current situation, and also revealed an unhealed event from her childhood:

Loss of Purpose
Fran Ayres

I look out across a grassy area to a small hill. On top of it is a round table covered with a tablecloth. The hill is not much bigger in circumference than the table. There is one empty chair, and on the other side of the table is another chair with a little white dog sitting on it. Then the dog falls off the chair and rolls down the hill.

"My job and my career had been very important to me," said Fran, "even to the point of being my identity at times. At retirement, I felt like I 'fell off' my place at the table of work, and the dog's downward tumbling represents my feelings of aimlessness and loss of purpose." Interestingly the size of the hill itself (her workplace) is so small that it provides no real grounding for the dog to stand on once it falls off the chair. It's simply all downhill from there.

Fran also saw another level of meaning in her dream. "In the previous year, I had completed a three-year spiritual direction training where I'd experienced much spiritual growth. When it ended, I felt adrift, missing the stimulation of the classes and the close bond of friendship with others in the training." No wonder her enthusiasm for life and her energy (the little dog) simply fell off and rolled away.

But the Dream Maker wasn't yet finished. Fran received the following dream only a few days later:

Breaking Out
Fran Ayres

I am in my kitchen. My co-worker Jan has left her dog with me. It's all white and medium-to-large in size. The dog has just had a bath, I think, because its fur looks so clean and fluffy. I want the dog to sit on the floor over by the sink. I tell it to go there by pointing in that direction. It runs over there but then jumps up on the counter and leaps through the window. The window was open, but the dog went right through the screen, tearing a big hole in it.

In contrast to Fran's introverted nature, her highly sociable co-worker Jan led an extravert's active life beyond their office. In this dream, Jan places her substantial energy (the dog) into the dreamer's care. Unlike Fran's previous dream dog, *this* energy is irrepressible. Instead of passively rolling downhill, this larger white dog points the way to a new perspective with considerable force. Jumping onto the forbidden territory of the kitchen counter, it leaps through a screen to freedom.

Fran understood the dog's clean fluffiness as her own fresh, new feelings about "a clean slate with no more workday schedules." It also presaged the condition of her soul in an upcoming waking life venture. "During the first six months of my retirement, I began volunteering at a start-up counseling center for body, mind and spirit. The environment was communal and supportive, something I'd not experienced in my previous work life. There was much affirmation of my work and appreciation for who I was and what I brought to the organization. It felt fresh and comfortable and I experienced new freedom to be creative."

In reflection, Fran felt her dream urging her to claim all her internal boldness (her friend Jan) and energy (the dog) to break through previously self-imposed barriers into a place of growth and community.

Another view of this dream emerged from Fran's reading of Ted Andrews' book *Animal Speak*[2], where she learned that it takes a great deal to break a dog's spirit. "When my confidence wavers, I remember that I do not have to leave (jump out a window). I can stay on my home ground as a faithful dog does, no matter where my feelings are trying to lead me." Aware that dogs often represent faithful, protective guides in dreams, she was gradually gaining confidence in her spiritual direction ministry, seeing herself as a faithful guide for others.

Illustrating the principle that dreams often have multiple levels of meaning, Fran realized that her two white dream dogs also pointed her toward a long-avoided issue from her past. "As a young girl, I experienced several losses," she said. "One of these was losing my childhood friend and pet, Fritzie. He just disappeared one day." Fran still treasures a photo of her three-year-old self hugging Fritzie, a white dog of an unknown breed with a brown face and a white blaze on his nose.

For years, she was unable to access her feelings about this painful event. "I must have walled them off. Fritzie was very important to me and his disappearance tore a big hole in my heart. I learned many years later that Fritzie was old and probably very sick. My dad did what most farmers in the country do with a sick, aged dog. They take them out in the woods and shoot them. When I learned that, I was angry, hurt and sad."

As Fran pondered her dreams and her childhood memory, she had a synchronous sighting of a dog resembling Fritzie as she drove home from church one day. This helped her to access and move into the healing first offered to her by the appearance of two white dogs in her dream world.

In my own life, I have had three dogs with whom I had close bonds – my beloved childhood mutt Cookie; the loving mixed-breed Tiger, the companion to my two children; and Shortcake, the beautiful black Great Dane I shared with a former husband. Despite loving each of these dogs deeply, I've always been more attuned to cats, so I pay special attention to my relatively infrequent dog dreams. They invariably point out something that I need to see.

The following three dreams offered me widely differing messages. The first, from an early journal, began tilling the ground, preparing me for future work:

A Man and Three Dogs

I'm in a room with a man and three dogs. He seems to be training them on the far side of a narrow bed. I am crouched down on the other side of the bed, watching. I can't see much of what is going on, but one dog with its back to me seems huge, about 200 pounds. I say quietly, "I'm afraid of your dogs." But the man doesn't hear me. I'm very apprehensive.

The bed, normally a place of rest, safety and security provides a scant barrier between me and the masculine figure who is managing the unfamiliar, frightening, instincts. My quiet words speak volumes about my timidity. Obviously, I have some inner work to do as this worrisome small dream reveals.

A second dream from the same period couples the dog with its wild cousin:

Two Pups in the Road

Two puppies are playing joyfully in the road, chasing each other and tumbling together. Then I see that one is a gray wolf pup and the other a yellow lab pup. All this is going on in front of the car, their energetic play moving along ahead of me as I drive.

While it's unclear whether I'm the driver or merely a passenger in this little dream, it contains a message that makes me smile. Knowing myself to be somewhat intense and serious in my waking world, here I receive a vision of what might be. The presence of wild and domestic energies, even the contrasting colors, suggest inner conflict as well as potential integration, with a healthier new balance of work and play. The happy scene of the two youngsters shows that I might also open up to more enthusiasm and fun without my forward progress in life and work grinding to a stop.

In contrast, the following dream came many years later during the COVID-19 pandemic. It arrived as a wonderous blessing during my intentional exploration of animal energies for this book:

The Rescue Dog

I'm outdoors in a street near a recovery center and dog rescue facility. I'm talking with a pleasant man from the recovery center. He seems to be doing well and I know he loves dogs. I ask, "How are you doing, being next door to the dogs?"

He says, "They were going to give me a dog but ...." and goes on to explain how it didn't work out.

Then I am lying down and a large black dog is lying peacefully on top of me, fully stretched out on his side with his head resting on my chest and neck. I am petting him, and his presence is wonderful. I feel deep joy and a connection that I've never experienced before.

Given the context of this dream – the internal and external turmoil of adjusting to the pandemic – this dream is remarkable, partly due to the dog's loving presence but also that I'm capable of feeling such wondrous joy in the encounter.

The adjacent recovery center and dog rescue facilities point toward my several decades in Twelve-Step recovery coupled with my love for animals. The dream also reminds me that, while I may attempt (and often would prefer) to intellectualize my way out of stress, sometimes I need to simply surrender (lie down) as I do here, relaxing into the encounter with something more mysterious (black) and profound than anything I've experienced before.

As I shared the dream with my spiritual director, we were both reminded of the words of a classic poem, *The Hound of Heaven*[3]:

> I fled Him, down the nights and down the days;
> I fled Him, down the arches of the years;
> I fled Him, down the labyrinthine ways
> Of my own mind ...

During the early years of my life, I had indeed run from God. This dream was a warm and holy encounter, linking my faith, my recovery and my deep belief in dreams for healing and wellness. I was literally rescued from external stresses, covered over in love, warmed by mystery, mercy and grace.

Pause

*How do you feel about dogs as humans'
most closely bonded species?
What within your waking life is reflected by
the dogs who appear in your dreams?*

Horses: Nobility and Resilience

We're told across many, many different cosmologies that we didn't go and find the horse and domesticate them. The horse came to us as a sacred partner, as a spiritual sibling, to partner with us in ways that were important and meaningful to humanity. Now what we did, is we stuck them in front of a plow and put them in battlefields. But I'm not sure that's what was necessarily intended, especially based on what I see when people and horses come together in ... transformational contexts.

Kelly Wendorf

I was an ungainly sixteen-year-old, visiting family in Amarillo, when a placid rental horse, bored with hauling around a chubby greenhorn, turned resolutely toward the barn and, ignoring my frantic attempts to redirect his progress, nosed his way through a narrow opening and deftly left me straddling the wooden gate as he plodded barn-ward. I limped away from that embarrassment with a painful abrasion on one leg and a crumpled ego. Since then I've cheerfully left riding flesh and blood horses to folks with a genuine affinity for their equine nature.

"Why do you think you have so many horses in your dreams?" I once asked a friend. "What does horse mean to you?" Anticipating some psychological probing on her part as she pondered my question, I laughed in surprise at her answer. "Well," she said quite seriously, "maybe it's because I grew up on a horse farm in Kentucky."

Of course! Sometimes the first layer of a dream's truth is just that obvious. But as we saw with dog dreams, we mustn't brush off an animal appearance simply because of close acquaintance, relegating the creature to be part of the scenery. Our creatures always come with purpose.

Our first dream of *equus caballus* comes from a longtime horsewoman familiar with grooming, tending and riding in competition, who has also cared for abused and neglected animals through *Habitat for Horses*[1]. Her dream reflects this deep kinship:

Let the Horses Run Free
Lanelle H.

I am walking in the nursery department of Home Depot and the aisles are crowded with new stock of painting supplies and various other things that have nothing to do with plants. I see a couple of paintbrushes that look like I might want them for my current painting project (in real life) in my bathroom, except I look at them with thoughts of stealing them. I pick them up and move through the aisles, wary of being seen.

The scene switches and I am leading two horses with ropes in a circular narrow path with wooden fences on both sides. We are walking abreast with them on my right, so it is difficult to navigate. Wide, strong ribbons of cloth or plastic are strung from side to side, tied to the fence rails about a horse length apart, so we have to duck under them. Some are so low it is difficult to get under them, which makes me frustrated. I question, in my mind, why on earth anyone would put those there. Of course, we continue to navigate the course in spite of the difficulties.

In processing this dream, Lanelle saw important similarities between the two dream segments – the crowded aisles of Home Depot and the narrow circular path she was following with the horses. Both segments contain elements that don't belong – first the painting supplies, then the ribbons. None appear in memorable colors.

While her dream begins in a setting of new growth (the nursery) and she finds supplies for brightening an inner place of cleansing (the paintbrush for her bathroom), she surreptitiously takes the brushes (perhaps she doesn't deserve them or can't pay for them) and moves away "wary of being seen." Lanelle sees this dream as connecting powerfully with a major transition in her career, in which she left her practice as a therapist to move into full-time ministry. There she felt far more exposed than when seeing clients in a private setting, and she was fearful about what others might say about her "being seen" in her new role.

The final sentence of the dream begins with "of course," pointing to the trait of persistence in the face of difficulties, which Lanelle said "is part of who I am." Her waking life challenges at the time of the dream included not only her career change but two significant medical issues with impending surgeries.

Lanelle acknowledged that she's always had abundant energy but keeps it tightly controlled. While her dream horses need no bridles or saddles, only simple ropes to guide them, they are snuggly confined in this image, tracing a mandala as they move counterclockwise encircling the divine center, her deepest Self.

For Lanelle, this dream embodies hope. Just as her processing reveals constraints within, it shows that the obstacles are only a horse length apart, something that she, an experienced horsewoman, can easily deal with. Together the three walk forward steadily, dipping below the obstacles on their way toward the instinctual resources that lie within.

Before sharing this dream, Lanelle had given it a tongue-in-cheek placeholder title: *What?* Responding to the projections of her dream group, Lanelle said, "I *love* the horse being my energy!" and unhesitatingly renamed her dream *Let the Horses Run Free*.

Our next dream comes from my daughter, who's always admired horses but had minimal contact with them in waking life. This gave her dream the special power of an unfamiliar encounter:

Two Healthy Horses
Kelly Bovier Stearman

I am walking in a see-for-miles country setting, when I see ahead a beautiful free horse, dark brown, almost black, unencumbered by human constraints. The horse is waiting for me, standing at an angle so it can easily look back at me. He's gazing right into my eyes, invitingly, as if speaking to me, saying, "Hurry up! Come on so we can run and play!" Ahead of the horse I see a large multi-use ranch trailer, similar to a horse trailer, but with rail sides and an open top.

Then I find myself walking toward two horses waiting for me – the same brown-black horse and a white horse he has brought with him. They stand side by side about three feet apart. They are both beautiful, with sleek, shiny coats and soft, flowing, long manes and tails. They are happy, healthy, peaceful and unconstrained.

I walk up to them from behind, thinking that I'm close enough to be kicked into eternity. Yet I feel no concern as I walk between them. They are relaxed, without tension, just waiting for me and enjoying my love as my hands touch their sides. I move toward their heads to love them. Everything feels serene, peaceful and expansive, with infinite possibilities in every direction.

At the time of this dream, Kelly had just returned to Texas and her family after a long journey up and down the west coast. For several years she had followed a semi-nomadic lifestyle, moving about the U.S., following or seeking job opportunities. To friends and family, her solo relocations and travels have often appeared bold and risky.

Kelly's experience of this dream centers on confirmation and assurance that she already possesses all that this beautiful pair of horses represent – power and freedom as well as the ability to travel. The horses are entirely free, lacking restraints. Even the ranch trailer expresses a message of freedom, its open top suggesting open options in life, "the sky's the limit," so to speak.

As a non-country-girl, Kelly nevertheless feels compelling invitation, even from a distance, as the first horse beckons with its eyes – a deeply connective gaze. Moving between the two strong animals, she feels a depth of soul from the dark horse and spiritual presence from the white horse. Her walk between them brings the two energies toward unification. When she comes to their heads, she said, "I can imagine reaching up with both hands and drawing the horses' heads toward mine."

Kelly experienced this dream as confirmation of who she already was, as well as a revelation of her power manifested in the horses. "I felt the energy of love passing back and forth between us," she said. The dream's words "close enough to be kicked into eternity" also suggest that her horses form a pathway to the divine.

New dreamworker Linda Hand accepted the invitation to share her powerful dream encounters with a beloved horse named Quick Silver who had, over the 18 years of life they shared, touched her at great depth.

The recent decades of Linda's life have been largely focused on inner healing of her painful childhood. She has pursued a variety of paths toward wholeness in addition to serving others through inner healing retreats and individual spiritual direction.

Here is Linda's story of Quick Silver: "My mother passed away in 1990, but it took years to probate the complicated and painful family history that was held in her will." When her two daughters finally received their shares of the estate, the younger, sixteen-year-old daughter chose to buy a horse.

"I had longed to own a horse when I was young and through many years of my adult life," said Linda. "But we didn't realize what it really took to have a horse, love it and take care of it." Over the next few years, she and her daughter shared the care for Quick Silver, a beautiful gray, spotted quarter horse. By the time Linda and her husband built a home on acreage where Silver could move from a rental barn to his own one-stall barn, her daughter was married, so Linda assumed all of Silver's care.

"Silver always knew the voice of his master – whether mine or my daughter's – and he was always thrilled with her visits and her children's." Then Silver developed Equine Cushing's Disease, which caused a range of troubling symptoms that Linda and her husband lovingly tended. "Silver was beautiful," said Linda, "and the daily care for him was pure mystery. Sometimes as I groomed him and braided his mane and tail, an owl watched from a nearby tree and let me talk to him." A strange and mystical appearance for the nocturnal owl.

Yet Silver was more than a beloved creature needing care; he was also Linda's healer. "My being with him throughout the ten years that he lived in our pasture was pivotal for my healing. I wonder if, in an empathic sense, my healing with Silver is transmitting to my ego a wider vision of our quantum entanglement, of all creation being interconnected, that allows us to help heal each other through our energy, even in dreams."

Although Silver died in 2010, his spirit lives on as shown in the following three dreams which Linda had nine years later over a three-month period:

Connected Inner Healing
Linda Hand

I am in a dwelling and Silver is in a huge square cage with legs that reminds me of a birdcage. Silver is full of sensitivity and I feel deep concern about him and the cage. I'm talking to someone about whether or not we should take the legs off the cage. Then the legs are off of the cage. At first, I care for Silver there and clean the cage. Then I'm caring for Silver when he's out of the cage – grooming, combing and brushing him, cleaning his hooves and feeding him hay and water.

Change of scene: I am providing medical care for a person who seems similar to one of the sisters at the Cenacle. This seems odd to me as I am not trained in medical care.

Dream Animal Wisdom

Notice that Linda's powerful instinct represented by Silver is at first confined as if it might walk away (legs on the cage) or fly away (birdcage similarity). But Linda engages this energy closely, both in and out of the cage, tending and feeding the beloved creature and fully integrating his available power.

Her understanding of Silver as a healer for her in waking life seems to carry over, once integrated, into her ability to offer healing to others in and through the spiritual community with which she was affiliated for years. She is shocked to recognize the woman who needed care – a sister who actually had many real-life health issues – but whom Linda found hard to like and who didn't seem to favor Linda at all. Here, Linda is given the opportunity to consider what rejected part of herself is ready to emerge for deeper healing. And how is she being offered the chance to claim her ability as a healer?

Linda received a second dream of Silver a month later:

Sacred Elements
Linda Hand

I am looking out of a house at dusk when I see a car coming from the right across to the left in the front yard. The ground is wet, and the car begins to make ruts in the green grass as I watch. It makes a wide curve and turns left to head behind the house. I notice the tire tracks in the soft, moist grass. Then the car is going fast, heading toward the stall where Silver is standing. The car swipes the stall and the stall catches fire. As I try to save Silver, the surroundings get darker.

Then I'm with Silver at the back of the pasture, away from the stall. It's still dark, but I'm relieved we are safe as I awaken.

Here we see a wide circular image as a car (means of moving through life) makes a sweeping arc around Linda's house (her life/psyche). What unidentified part of the dreamer is at the wheel as this car speeds along and swipes Silver's stall? At the time of this dream, many family issues created an out-of-control feeling in Linda's waking life. Circumstances rushed along in a threatening way, damaging Linda's inner landscape and threatening to harm her most precious, powerful energy (Silver).

On another level, Linda accepts the sacramental aspects in the water present in the ground and in the burst of fire – the symbol of refinement or purification. "Brother horse, sister water," she said. Even in the darkness, all is well when she fully integrates her energy, and Linda was heartened by the positive ending of this dream.

Only two weeks later, she dreamed the following:

Practicing and Processing Healing
Linda Hand

I'm at my house with other people including my younger daughter. Silver, originally my daughter's horse, is hidden in a closet with a folded black cover over his head. He is not upset. I tell my daughter to bring Silver out and take the cover off his head. When the cover is set on the countertop, it becomes a carafe-like container. We then use the carafe to give him water and rinse him with it too.

I lean against Silver. I'm glad he was not upset about the closet and the cover over his head. Then my daughter and I notice his mane is grainy as if he'd rolled in damp sand and we begin bathing him. The texture of his mane is interesting with dark, grainy parts and smooth, lighter gray parts – a lot of contrast.

During the period of these dreams, Linda's inner work included sorting through 72 years of photographs, ridding herself of many childhood images. "That felt good!" she said, linking her waking life purging to cleansing the dark, grainy material from Silver's mane in the dream. This careful attention to the horse's mane also parallels the common symbolism of human hair as strength and virility, compounding the symbolic power of the horse itself.

As with the fire in her previous dream, Linda recognizes the strong sacramental aspect of the cover on Silver's head becoming a carafe for water used to cleanse him. In waking life, rinsing Silver was a frequent part of his care due to his disease, and here it represents a spiritual baptism.

Linda is touched by the presence of her daughter because of the love they shared for this beautiful horse. She feels that her daughter also represents her younger self, coming into this healing scene, partnering with her dream ego in the task of freeing up the energy embodied by Silver. The beloved horse seems happy and at ease with their loving care. "I also know in my heart the symbolism of the animal, the water, and other elements are very trinitarian," Linda said.

As Linda seeks to more fully understand her dreams, significant integration of energy seems to be taking place. Although Quick Silver died a decade ago, he lives on within Linda as a beloved companion healer. "Silver was so important to me that I was very disciplined about his care. I notice that in most of my dreams about him, one of us is trying to take care of the other." Linda added that healing is not a simple, once-and-for-all process. "It's the practice and process of a lifetime. I'm still contemplating these dreams in my soul and I have the feeling that all is well."

Pause

*When has your heart been touched by
horses – in books, in movies, in life?
What dream horses have emerged from your
personal experience or imagination?*

Cats: Creatures of My Heart

*A cat has absolute emotional honesty:
human beings, for one reason or another, may hide their feelings,
but a cat does not.*

Ernest Hemingway

Combing through my dream journals for animal appearances, I made the startling discovery of more than 70 dreams in which domestic cats appeared. Sometimes they played minor walk-on parts and in others, they claimed starring roles. Ironically the only journal devoid of *felis catus* dreams was a slender softbound notebook loaded with cat illustrations and printed quotes.

Cats are integral to my inner landscape as well as my waking life, which I have almost continuously shared with feline companions. And I have plenty of photos to memorialize a wonderful pilgrimage to London's British Museum where, in the Egyptian section, I stood grinning helplessly besides a glorious bronze cat statue, a glass case of cat mummies, a trio of massive, enthroned cat-headed deities. It was as if I'd finally reached the headwaters of my personal psychic river.

For the reader who may not be fond of cats, I entreat you to stay the course through this chapter. You may find some of my processing transferrable to whatever creature's heart is beating in your dream world.

My earliest work with dream cats, while sincere and enthusiastic, was hampered by inexperience and frustrated by the typical symbolic linkage of cat with the sensual and the feminine which seemed overly simplistic and didn't quite fit.

Here is the first major appearance of the cat on my dream stage, a profound early encounter:

The White Cat and the Insect Queen

I am aware of an insect queen who attracts all the insects to her to draw sustenance. A man tells me I can see her from where I am. So I kneel to peer under a low obstacle where I can see her plump, larva-like white shape.

Suddenly the scene shifts and I'm in an outdoor space. In a central area, I see a white cat with a collar, sitting beside the insect queen, who is about half as big as the cat. Off to the left, not far away, are two or three other white cats at rest.

This 2005 dream has resonated through the years as *my wisdom cat* appearance. I simply *knew* the importance of this white cat, sitting there in the sacred center (my Self, where I meet the divine). Revisiting the written dream, I rediscover the podgy, larval-like, stark white insect queen, with her deep, primal, primitive energy, an embryonic promise of the archetype within. The cat, wearing a collar to let me know she belongs to me, stands sentry beside this outsized nurturing, mothering energy. Today I see this dream encompassing both queen and the great mother, Sophia, and I recognize it as even more foundational in my journey of individuation than it appeared to me years ago.

So what has this amazingly persistent creature been coming to convey to me? As the most prevalent creature in my dream animal pantheon, Cat opened the way for other energies on the prowl within me and showed me the value of an open channel to the unconscious and the riches that lay in wait for me there. From the beginning, Cat has been pointing out my need for psychospiritual healing and integration.

Early on, my psyche took full advantage of my compassion for helpless, wounded and neglected creatures, delivering up the sort of distressing images that often cause new dreamworkers to shiver and slam the lid down on a dream the minute they awaken. It was a tremendous relief for me to learn that suffering animals represent some aspect of myself. Frankly, it was more comfortable for me to accept that an unconscious part of me was in pain or neglected than it was to think about an animal in distress ... even an imaginary one. That awareness then allowed me to open to a previously unknown need for inner healing. It was a wake-up call to my need for better self-care.

It's quite probable that compassionate readers who've been tending dreams for a time can recall vivid suffering creature scenes of their own. So I will summarize just a few such dream images to make my point: *I find a weak, starving kitten covered with parasites and I determine to take it to a vet for treatment. I discover a tiny kitten about to drown in a bowl of mushy, tan-colored cat food and I scoop it out, intending to wash it and save it. A woman who wants to get rid of her huge cat tosses it aside and the cat simply lies there staring at me.* All of these images urge me to ask what within me has been unrecognized, neglected or cast aside with such disregard?

Over time, I could see my dream cats becoming more personal to me, taking on the personalities of some of my housecats and feral cats. Consider the following dream that begins with Mr. White, a sweet, shy member of one of the community cat colonies I tend:

Injured Cats

I am looking out a window when I see Mr. White dash across the street between two cars. I can see he's been hit because he leaves the road limping and staggering. I go outside to find and help him. To my surprise, I instead find two other unhealthy feral cats lying stretched out, side by side. I think one is dead, but when I touch it, it sits up to be greeted and petted. They both have wounds that need veterinary care. Someone tells me that they've been living around there for a long time.

Here the cat I know leads me deeper within to two other cats I don't yet know. The two vehicles (my way of moving through life) and the two other cats (parts that, like Mr. White, have been injured by my manner of living) represent choices and my need for balance. Significantly the cat that appears lifeless responds quickly, positively to human touch. The wisdom voice tells me that these two, unknown, unhealthy cats have been living within me for a long time. Now that I know these energies are present, I can look for help (my dream ego often thinks about seeking veterinary care for my dream animals). The task suggested by this dream is to pursue my development and healing by welcoming the instinctual energies that lie within, which have been languishing without adequate self-care.

A second personal theme is vividly illustrated by my *caged and controlled* cat dreams. During the summer when I was most actively involved in the Trap-Neuter-Return program, my dreams underscored my exasperating need to be in control – not only of the neighborhood population of feral cats but also of my psychic energies. For example: *Several cats are neatly organized on individual placemats (all in their places) in a cupboard.* In another dream: *A man pries the lid off a thick wooden box to release a cat that's been scratching inside. The box contains food, water and bedding, but it's a prison nonetheless.*

Given such dreams about restraint, I was delighted with the following movement toward hope. Each of these dream cats has a room with a view!

Rentals for Cats

I'm in a large room surrounded by windows with box enclosures for cats installed at each window, giving each cat a view of the outdoors. These are rentals. One special box on the left wall extends out from the building, allowing the cat in it to gaze out in multiple directions. It has a higher rental cost than the enclosures against the flat windows. I am surprised and impressed with this place!

I still chuckle at my psyche's determination to loosen me up a little. But I see no storage cupboards with placemats or rough-hewn boxes here, only well-constructed, light-filled rental spaces for which an owner (me) is willing to pay well. A part of me has already paid a premium for greater vision.

From this point forward I notice movement beyond cautions about self-care and commentary on my overly organized nature. My dream cats began to offer new lessons, more complex and sophisticated messages.

If I were to list my favorite cat dreams, the following would rank among the top five. It erupted with all the force, clarity and memorability of a Big Dream, becoming the pivot point for my understanding of the differing energies of housecats and feral cats and what they signify about my Self:

Cats from the Deep

I am seated outdoors in a parking lot beside a building, surrounded by many cats that I know are mine. Suddenly something disturbs the cats who live in a deep place under the building to my right. They come rushing out, angry and dangerous, running across in front of me to the left. I see two scruffy black cats among them. They don't attack or menace me or any of my cats. But I'm disturbed.

Just as the threat seems to subside, the cats from the deep return, moving back to where they came from. My cats want to interact with them, especially a small calico kitten among them. But I'm still cautious. "Don't try to make friends with them!" I say to my cats. I don't know or trust the cats from the deep.

From its peaceful beginning, this dream quickly becomes unsettling. I'm filled with a sense of danger as unknown cats living under the building literally pour across my field of view. When they begin flowing back in the direction from which they came, the dream offers the sweet gift of an appealing, friendly calico kitten. Yet I fear even that unsullied little creature. I awakened chagrined by my timidity and reluctance to engage this roiling mass of deeper instincts.

This dream, in fact, takes me into my past and provides new awareness. The building under which these unknown dream cats live is the actual building where I attended my earliest Twelve-Step recovery meetings. This setting tells me that, regardless of all my previous inner work, much more remains to be discovered and these unacknowledged instincts emerging in feral attire seem dangerous because of their repression. The scruffy black cats, the least known, most frightening parts of my shadow, remind me that I *must* have the courage to make friends with these forces or they will simply scramble back into hiding to surge forth at a later time, more unkempt and demanding of attention than before.

Cats from the Deep was significant in another way as well. I had just accomplished multilayered processing of my early turtle dreams (see *Turtle* chapter) and I suppose I assumed that my work with one animal energy would fully explain another. This dream, however, helped me realize that my dream cats had a distinct array of messages to communicate.

Fortunately, other dreams began showing my ego the way to relax my tight grip on all aspects of my life. One night at a dream conference, after the day's probing discussions stirred up my unconscious, I dreamed this:

The Cats are Out

I'm in my house and discover that the sliding glass door that opens to the backyard is wide open and I'm sure all of my housecats have gotten outside. Worried, I go out into the expansive yard with its verdant green, inviting grass. I see all five cats off to the right, sitting in a circular pattern. They are simply enjoying the freedom and the outdoor view.

I call and one of the males gets up and comes toward me. I pick him up and hold him to my chest. Then I see Pebbles, the female, looking at me and beginning to move in my direction. I realize that if I walk back to the house, the other cats will all come and follow me inside.

What new freedom! For the first time, I dream of my waking life *indoor* cats. Finding them outside, I'm concerned but not frantic. Instead, I feel calmly confident that they will follow me back inside. This affirming dream recognizes my progress in releasing the need to keep my energies in check. It's also noteworthy that the cats on the lush lawn (green for hope and growth) arrange themselves in a mandala, surrounding my Self.

This awareness helped to set the inner dream stage for what was to come, moving beyond knowing the cat as my personal wisdom figure and conveyor of self-help messages, to welcoming Cat as archetype, crone and the divine feminine:

The Old Lady's Cat

I am with one of the pastors of my church in the tiny, cramped house of an old woman. I'm aware of the pastor and the old woman standing at my left and a recliner on my right. I reach down between the chair back and the seat where there's a pocket of cloth. I feel something soft and I think it must be things that have fallen and collected there. To my surprise, I pull out a cat! The cat is small – only six to eight pounds – a deep red-orange tabby. She seems healthy, but maybe a little undernourished. She's apprehensive about being pulled out of hiding into the light. If she were mine, I think, I would take care of her and feed her well.

This dream is a story of finding treasure, a hidden energy that my crone self (the old woman) knows about, but my ego doesn't. My pastor friend's presence lends spiritual authority to the visit. He and the woman, both elderly, signify an integration of elder wisdom, standing on my intuitive side. When I turn to the right and pull out the cat, I bring forgotten, stifled energy into consciousness. The tabby's pronounced color underscores the excitement and hopefulness of the discovery; her color is even more significant since orange tabbies are typically male. By finding and retrieving this bright cat, I reclaim (and can now nourish) another hidden part of myself.

A humorous aspect of this dream is that I am older than my pastor and probably the same age as the "old woman," which underscores that it's never too late to face reality, for a woman to acknowledge her crone self and embrace new energy for the wonders that lie ahead.

To conclude this chapter I offer a dream in which a dear friend teams up with a group of cats for a meaningful advance in my spiritual journey:

Becky's Cats

I am in Becky's big complex house to attend a meeting, but I am delayed somehow and can't keep up with the others. When I finally locate and enter the room at the end of a long hall, I see Becky and the other women already seated in comfortable chairs around the room. It's a warm, inviting corner room with many pieces of furniture and a homey atmosphere. Becky welcomes me with words like, "Here she is" and a warm smile. Yet I feel reluctant to cross the room and take a chair. I feel out of place, like I don't fit in.

Time shifts ahead and I'm in the same room alone with Becky and her big resting cats. The seven cats are all large and healthy, lying in comfortable places on furniture around the room. I pause just inside the door, observing one big cat who is in a bed that happens to be right at the level of my heart.

❣

Whenever I encounter Becky in a dream, I know soul work is underway. This dream had a powerful effect and felt like recurring dream material, which isn't surprising since it points to a familiar issue – my persistent sense of lagging behind everyone else in the spiritual communities within which I work and thrive.

Becky is one of my most admired spiritual mentors and, as a result, a great deal of my psychic stuff has constellated around her into a "spiritual mentor complex" (her complex house) into which I have funneled both authority and proficiency in spiritual direction and spiritual formation activities. This dream highlights the part of me that still feels I haven't quite earned my place in this company of women. I understand that bright shadow is at work here too; I've projected much of my competence onto my unsuspecting friend.

In the first segment of the dream, after an unspecified delay, I find the room at last. The shift to the second scene is momentous when all the fragments of me (the other women) fade away or move into integration. In the second part, I know I *do* fit in. This corner room with windows on two sides offers new perspectives. And here resides powerful feminine energy embodied seven times over in these big healthy cats – bringing in the sacred number for human wholeness and the cycle of life.

I even meet the great mother here – Sophia in Becky guise. Sitting calmly to my right, she simply receives and welcomes me: "Here she is." Revisiting this dream scene, I hear in my soul that it's time to stop apologizing about my presence in any setting and about what I have or haven't accomplished in my life and spiritual growth.

Seeing how this deep issue erupted in this dream, I allowed it to play out into healing by reentering the dream in active imagination (see *Appendix III*): *I pause in the doorway of this room at the end of the long passage. Then I step forward to claim my place. I turn* about slowly in the center of the room, knowing that I can look out the windows and see unlimited vistas. But now is a time to remain within. I choose a comfy chair and sit amidst the pillows. One by one the handsome cats come to me, purring vibrant energy into me as they take places on my lap, at my sides, on the back of my chair. I sense the shimmering presence of Sophia across from me and I close my eyes to float in the purring and kneading of my deep feline essence, sitting in my chair in my inner room, a sacred place with unlimited possibilities.

Pause

What special animal comes to you as a recurring nighttime visitor? How have your dream creature's messages evolved over time?

Cats: The Wild Ones

*The history of the cat family can be traced back to fossil ancestors
that already appeared catlike about 37 million years ago.
Today's 37 species range from small cats to the big, wild, roaring creatures.*

Britannica

When I was old enough to earn my own money and began buying books (a habit in which I still eagerly indulge), one of my first purchases was a beautiful volume of photos and text about the world's big cats. These great wild cats open up a world that doesn't depend upon a connection to (or even much appreciation for) the domestic housecat. Some engender awe for their size and strength, others for their mysterious, solitary behavior, some for their enthralling beauty. Feline energy is so common in dreams that the wild ones deserve this chapter of their own.

Robert Johnson, author of the classic *Inner Work*[1], tells an amusing, instructive story about his frightening encounter with a dream lion. After four sessions of active imagination failed to resolve the troubling dream, he finally realized that the lion wasn't harming him. This belated awareness freed him to explore why his lion had come to him. Lions and tigers make some major appearances in Part II; here we will meet a variety of other creatures.

Our first dream shows how the briefest of images may signal that something new is afoot. Even how a creature materializes can be a significant part of the message. This is the experience of dreamworker and photographer Lisa Rigge who encountered one of the wild cats unique to North America:

Bobcat Appears
Lisa Rigge

I am looking into a river of trees, staring into its depths although I can't make out anything. Then a bobcat morphs into view. It's still mostly hidden by the trees, but undoubtedly a bobcat.

❦

"That I remembered this dream years later tells of its impact on me," Lisa said. "I knew it was important as I'd never dreamed of a bobcat, nor of any animal that was first hidden and then seen." Explaining how the bobcat appeared gradually, she said, "It was like a Bev Doolittle camouflage painting[2] that you need to look at carefully before you can see the animal. It was a slow awakening and recognition that something was there." It also represented the patience a dreamer needs to see what is coming from the unconscious.

In her dream, the *river of trees* holds special energy. "It's a lovely place, like a forest river with so many trees that it's hard to distinguish one from another. To look into the depths of the forest is to become aware of what it has to offer. It's to be silent, to listen, to discern what is actually there. My feeling is one of mystery, awe and curiosity." She added, "The forest depths also refer to the depths of oneself – depths that one reaches when meditating, writing or creating art when one is alone and discovers new places in herself or the world at large."

Embracing the strength of her bobcat symbol, Lisa set out to explore it first with creative expression rather than intellectual analysis. As a photographer and collage artist, she followed her natural path of imagery to bring the dream into her waking environment. She experimented with photos and Internet images and eventually took a drawing class, hoping to bring forth her personal bobcat. Yet nothing fully captured what she sensed just beyond her reach, and bobcat sank back into a waiting mode in her unconscious.

Three years later, bobcat returned:

Cat and Bobcat
Lisa Rigge

I'm outdoors with a few people from church when I look into the leaves and brush at the side of the road and see a bit of movement – more than the wind would make. As I look, I see the head of a black cat. The bushes quiver even more, shake a bit, but only in the area I'm watching. Then a bobcat emerges from the undergrowth. I have some fear – more like amazement – as it walks up the small hillside by the road. I feel no need to shout out a warning to the others who are with me.

♥

In her dream, Lisa doesn't draw attention to the bobcat. Instead, she feels that she is the only one who sees it, confirming that the creature has come to her, and only to her. She also feels that the unusual wind is spiritual, "something trying to get my attention," which is further emphasized by the bobcat "walking up the hill, an ascension."

For Lisa the black cat which first appears points toward the feminine. As cat becomes bobcat, she sees the transformation from domestic to wild, instinctual cat, while *Bob*, the name of her deceased brother, indicates an integration of masculine and feminine. Yet even this awareness didn't fully bring the creature to light.

At this point, Lisa reengaged her bobcat with determination, examining her subjective associations, discussing the dream with her spiritual director and studying the nature of bobcat itself. In reading Ted Andrews' *Animal Speak*, she quickly grasped the strong affinity between the bobcat's typically solitary nature and her own. Like the bobcat, who often remains hidden while observing others, Lisa acknowledged that she keeps much of herself hidden from others until friends who know her well "draw me out of hiding into a safe place to bare my soul."

Her research also led her to understand the wind as both an agent of change and the spirit of life moving one through experiences. "I sense that, yes, I've been through internal changes toward ideas and beliefs that are more in service to Self." She sees the reality of change in recent successes – publishing her article about bobcat[3] and having photos accepted by a respected photography magazine. "Perhaps I need to get used to and celebrate these successes!" she said, acknowledging new confidence in her ability to move forward with her goals.

As life would have it, Lisa was blessed with a synchronous sighting of a bobcat as she and her husband hiked the hills near their California home. The big cat paused and looked directly at her, allowing her to view and photograph it. Then it padded away through tall grasses to a rocky ridge where Lisa imagined a litter of cubs may have waited. This led to a poignant *ah-ha* as she reflected upon a female bobcat raising her cubs alone and her own childhood with a mostly absent father.

Throughout the processing of her bobcat dreams, Lisa has been gently guided to a far deeper understanding of why and how this particular creature has appeared to her. She sees it emerging from both the personal and collective unconscious. For Lisa, bobcat has come as itself and as a composite of her masculine and feminine energies, bringing forth material from her past and revealing and confirming who she is in her solitary, patient way, allowing her to live her life more deeply than ever before.

I invite you now into a pair of big cat dreams shared by a close friend and fellow dreamworker who's been blessed with numerous big cat appearances. In this first dream she encounters a leopard and makes a visit to the sacred center:

Dream Animal Wisdom

The Leopard and the Fire
Margie O.

I am driving down a road with woods on both sides. There are others in the car with me, including my daughter Lisa, as a child. Then I am in the rear passenger seat with the window rolled down. Suddenly a leopard leaps through the open window. I'm startled and I reflexively push it out, but it runs along beside the car and leaps in again. It starts to purr and I stroke his shoulders and back and scratch behind his ears. He continues to lean against me, purring.

Then we're all out of the car and have ventured into the woods. After a while, we realize the woods are on fire. We try to leave but the fire has encircled us and there is no way out. The circle has not yet closed in when a helicopter hovers above us and moves downward to land. Everyone else gets into the helicopter but there is not enough room for me. I want to make sure the others get away. They are crying and the pilot tells them he will come back for me. But he and I look at each other, both knowing there won't be enough time for him to make it back for me. I wave goodbye as the helicopter takes off. I am sad but grateful that they got out.

Knowing Margie as an extraordinary caregiver, steadfast in her love for a wide network of family members, foster children and the children in a South American country she visits on mission trips, I can envision her making such a selfless sacrifice as this dream portrays.

In the beginning of the dream, Margie feels peaceful and in control (driving her car). "The trees that line both sides of the road represent my family history," she said, "the core of who I am, and the balance of traits that I have gained from both my parents." The presence of her daughter (her own young self) invites her to examine her childhood and to explore old feelings of inadequacy that have shadowed her for decades. In the shift to the rear passenger seat, she interprets a need to release control so she may see how she's been living. "The window is rolled down, so all barriers have been removed," she said. "I can see clearly now."

Enter the leopard, powerful and majestic, leaping through the open car window. "I'm shown that the strength of the leopard, God's power, is within me if I will accept it," she said. "This is my opportunity to reclaim lost power, to accept 'my spots' and use them as my strength." Though she resists at first (shoving the leopard back out the window), this formidable instinct keeps pace with the car and muscles its way back in. This time, Margie receives it. "I am willing to embrace it and I'm comfortable and confident. I feel myself and the leopard becoming one as it purrs and leans into me. This assures me that I have all the power and strength needed to accomplish my goals."

With the change of scene, still surrounded by the trees, "all that makes me who I am," Margie continues her journey of transformation. As the fire closes in, the negative aspects of her mother complex, the "smother mother," swoops in as a descending helicopter, driving her deeper into unconscious material and bringing the insight that old tapes and old ways of being have been stifling her.

Margie sees those who accompany her on this journey as aspects of herself that she needs to shed. "Part of me (the pilot) wants to rescue all these parts of me, but I know I need to release them, so I look him in the eye and wave goodbye. The stripped-down core of me cannot go and I'm sad. It's as if a big part of who I have been is leaving. The separation of Self is hard to do but I'm grateful I can let them go."

The steadily encroaching circular fire leaves no way out. "The fire is a means of purification that allows the negative words and feelings of my past to be consumed, leaving only what is good and helpful. There is no way around this process." Divested of what no longer serves her, Margie is left alone in this process of personal transformation, in the center, a flame-bounded mandala of her sacred Self.

Five years later another big cat stepped forth in this dream:

Retreat with the Cougar
Margie O.

I'm on a retreat with a group of women and we're getting ready to go on a sight-seeing bus trip. The retreat leader has beautiful, multicolored, flowing tops for all of us. I pick one with blues and greens that I like. The ladies try on different ones – some of them are taking forever, changing their minds and getting sidetracked as we get dressed to go.

The bus is like a yellow school bus and the windows are open halfway. I sit near the back so I can focus on the surroundings. The area looks like Yellowstone with beautiful scenery and wide-open spaces. The women in the front of the bus are visiting and not really interested in the sights around them. I don't feel like a part of this group. I just don't seem to fit in.

We are traveling in a large circle around the park, a trip that takes all day. In the late afternoon, we cross a long bridge over a river with small, branching streams and enter a wooded area. Driving along, we see a cougar and stop to get a better look. The women up front say, "Oh, look! A cougar!" and go right back to their visiting. The cougar comes up to my window and I reach out to stroke this beautiful cat. I keep stroking his soft grey-brown fur and he turns his head all around for me to keep doing it.

The bus starts up again and we continue on. When we get back to our dormitory it's almost dark. We all get off the bus and the other women go inside. But I see movement in the trees off to the right of the bus. It's the cougar! It has followed us all the way back. I walk to the tree line and the cougar approaches me. I sit down on the ground and he lays down and puts his head and paws in my lap. I sit talking to him and stroking him as he purrs and looks at me with his big, beautiful, expressive green eyes.

This dream's opening bristles with annoyance and frustration. Margie doesn't feel a part of this group – women who are more interested in how they look (taking a long time to choose their attire) and in chit-chat than in enjoying the wonder of their surroundings. "Everything about them is gossipy and cliquish," Margie said. "On the bus, they group together visiting, ignoring all the beauty around us." The dream also highlights Margie's intuitive nature and interest in the more meaningful things of life "as opposed to talking about nothing, which doesn't really form relationships."

The dream also offers encouragement "to go off and find quiet time with nature instead of always being in the rush and busyness of daily life." Meanwhile, the references to yellow (the bus and the park itself) point her toward new openings and possibilities.

Margie sees the bus itself as an apt metaphor for psyche with the women at the front representing an unattractive part of the collective and her consciousness, and her place at the back, representing the unconscious. Notice that she has chosen the blue/green colored top to wear – favorite, soothing colors that speak to her of water. Traveling in the bus, wearing her *flowing* top, she crosses a bridge (threshold) over a *flowing* river and branching streams, moving into a deeper place where she is ready for the encounter with cougar.

This cougar dream warrants comparison with Margie's leopard dream. Both dreams have a strong, circular mandala in conjunction with big cat energy. With these sleek power animals purring against her, Margie is centered in her authentic Self, the positive, powerful feminine – totally aside from her family and friends and even from the more frivolous manifestations of the feminine as represented by the other women on the bus in her first dream. "To be in one's center," Margie said, "one must be alone and at-one with the parts of ourselves so deep that they can only be expressed by animals."

♥

Sarah Norton, a long-time dedicated dreamworker with a Ph.D. in depth psychology[4], shares the following series of jaguar encounters.

"My initial dream with the jaguar came in the spring one of my more difficult years," she said. "I was deep master's degree program which soon after became my so I did not process the dream much at the time. Even so, the image stuck with me."

Previously she had associated the big cats with her best friend from youth because of his affinity for them. But her dream jaguar was different; it arrived as the divine feminine, embedded in a quest dream – a theme not uncommon to Sarah throughout her journey of individuation:

Castle Guards
Sarah D. Norton

I'm in a deep wood around a castle. I sense a jaguar nearby but have a sense it may just be a statue; it does not seem animate. I am running through the woods and barely miss a falling iron gate. I have an image of a lady in white who falls into a culvert nearby. Then I see a coiled white snake and a slithering black snake along my path.

I finally make it to the castle and another jaguar is there as if standing guard, so still, but poised to pounce. It is deep black with a hint of even deeper black spots somehow in its coat. Its eyes are piercing green. I realize the other jaguar I felt was a statue must have been similarly poised, and that both jaguars are vibrant and alive.

Suddenly a man jumps out at me with a knife. I am able to fend him off with a dagger of my own and I continue into the castle grounds knowing I need to find someone to tell me where I have come from and why I am there so they can help me complete my quest.

This dream languished, forgotten, for about four years, until Sarah took part in a guided meditation. Here is her experience:

Green Eyes
Sarah D. Norton

I am in a dark wood near a fire in a clearing. As I walk away from the fire I look beyond the trees and see the stars in the night sky ahead of me. The stars become eyes, green eyes in a dark, beautiful feline face. The jaguar stares at me through the branches, with leaves obscuring her fearsome jaw. The low rumble of her growl could almost be a purr. The whole Milky Way reflects in the pools of her dark green gaze.

"*I know you,*" *I say.* "*I have seen you in my dreams before.*"

"As soon as I saw the jaguar's green eyes, I remembered her," Sarah said. This reappearance prompted her into an active imagination process with her *Castle Guards* dream. "In active imagination, the jaguar began to lead me even more into the darkness, with her being punctuated by the light of the stars. Her green eyes called out to me as a message from the earth, reminding me that I am but one small piece of a vast ecosystem. The threat of her was now a comfort, her growl a purr. It seemed that her standing guard was not against me, but *for* me, and she had been waiting for me in that dream years ago. Now I saw her as standing guard at the border of the woods and outside the castle to make sure my path was clear."

The fact that her jaguar was black with even darker black spots was intriguing. Her research confirmed that what is often called a "black panther" is typically a leopard or jaguar with a gene that produces a dark pigment, hence her black jaguar. She was also aware of the mythological connections of jaguar with the Incas, which she remembered from her travel to Peru.

Of all its characteristics, the jaguar's green eyes were most absorbing. "I sat with those green eyes for quite some time," she said. An artist, she drew a compelling green eye surrounded by black fur, then examined her color associations. "Green feels very whole and numinous to me. It's also an exercise in contrast: there's the green of nature and of money, and there's the green of new life and of decay." She added that the green of public policy to address climate issues versus the monetary (green) profits of fossil fuels also ties in with the jaguar being a species inhabiting threatened rainforests. "In green, there is a great tension of opposites."

For Sarah, her dream jaguar was coming forward in a new, life-giving way. "It felt connected to the idea of the gold in the shadow, or the green sprouting seed in the dark soil, a sign of something poised on the threshold of being."

Two years later, another dream lifted jaguar to another level:

The Goddess
Sarah D. Norton

I'm in a town with a huge cathedral/temple. On top is a sculpture of the Norse goddess Frigg/Freyr with a large cat like a jaguar beside her. The white marble-like stone sculpture is huge – it towers above the town and can be seen from just about everywhere.

This dream underscores the feminine nature of Sarah's jaguar as well as the common association of big cats with certain goddesses. "I know it is my same black jaguar, but now she is set in white stone with her goddess beside her." Given her patrilineal ancestry from Norway, Sarah is especially inspired by Norse mythology. (See her *Go North!* dream in *Ancestral Callings*.) This dream setting reminds Sarah of Reykjavik, Iceland, a modern town with a sense of ancient Nordic roots. The massive sculpture that can be seen from afar fuses the qualities of two Norse goddesses: Frigg, the wife of Oden, skilled in magical arts and the archetypal mother; and Freyr, a wise warrior who is often compared to the Greek Artemis.

Appearing with this great composite goddess, "Jaguar has now risen to her archetypal status and is reaffirming in concrete terms her numinous power," Sarah said. "The mere image of her holds power and meaning. Her whiteness still holds the dark of the unconscious but has been brought into the light of consciousness. I know that she is there for me to connect to in a more intentional way now. When I need her energy to guide and protect me, it is there."

In reflecting upon her jaguar experience, particularly the first dream, Sarah was reminded of the powerful imagery of Jung's *Red Book*[5]. "The *Red Book* was the primary source for my dissertation," she said, "so it was in my consciousness a lot." Jung had included images that linked to her *Castle Guards* dream: the ancient knight (the man attacking her at the castle), the black and white snakes (in the forest), and a woman in white (the falling woman), which often appeared to Jung as his embodied soul. "The most interesting part is that I hadn't read those passages in the Red Book at the time of the *Castle Guards* dream. And I had been so focused on the jaguar that I didn't even recognize the rest of it!"

Regarding the underlying quest theme, Sarah said, "We know we are all on a journey that is life, hopefully, to find purpose and wholeness; but it's a journey that can never be completed during our lifetime and there is no definite direction. We do what we can with what we have and find our way through with purpose … but without a map."

Pause

What big dream cat has come to share its energy with you?
How does the nature, appearance and behavior
of this cat inform your dream?

Birds: On the Wing

*But ask the animals, and they will teach you,
or the birds of the air, and they will tell you.*

Bible - Job 12:7

Some years ago I planned my visits to family in the Pacific Northwest to coincide with spiritual opportunities at a lovely, wooded retreat center in Lacey, Washington. It helped my heart, saddened by my father's decline, to spend a day amidst the towering fir trees of my home country. I was still a wide-eyed novice dreamworker the day I entered a rustic building there to attend a workshop on animal dreams.

About two dozen seekers gathered around a Jungian analyst who created our sacred space then invited us to place our dream titles in a basket. The first dream selected was titled *Starving Parakeets*. After hearing the dreamer's poignant tale of finding emaciated parakeets in a forgotten room of her house, we learned that this woman had once raised parakeets. That moment concretized for me the principle that effective dreamwork should *always* begin with our personal associations. Just as Cat and Turtle were beginning to emerge as my soul-expressing creatures, for that dreamer, parakeets were the superlative metaphor for neglected fragments of her psyche.

Remarkably the 10,000 species of birds that co-exist with us in our modern world are most closely related to crocodilians; they are, in fact, feathered theropod dinosaurs! This deep grounding in earth's primal past creates intriguing contrast with the spiritual element that birds so often bring into our dreams. My own admiring-observer relationship with birds sometimes manifests in dreams with birds in the abstract rather than the flesh.

Whenever I'm away from home overnight on retreats, my dreams tend to be compelling in content and recall. In the wee hours of one such night, I climbed from bed in my stark little room to journal several dreams that culminated in this breathtaking image:

White Cloud Birds

I see in the sky two beautiful symmetrical birds, cranes, formed of lovely white clouds. As I look in wonder, I then see another perfect pair of cloud birds. I'm enchanted and amazed by their beauty.

Tall, leggy white cranes abound in the Galveston Bay area southeast of Houston where I live. For me, these slow-stepping birds represent elegance and grace, and white clouds have always carried spiritual promise for my journey. I pay special heed to specific words that appear in my dream reports, and here I describe my cloud birds as *symmetrical*. So this simple image, incorporating the rich potential of the number two, represents emerging concepts. This entrancing moment of harmony and balance promises me even more – if I continue to watch and listen. What a lovely encounter with Spirit conveyed in the clouds.

Birds also appeared to me in abstract form, with quite a different message, in the following dream:

Tree with Paper Birds

I see a tree, like a triangular cardboard cutout or stage prop, with bird cutouts hanging from all its branches. At first, I'm looking at the base of the tree with birds in it. Then I raise my sights and see the middle of the tree with many more birds. Finally, I raise my sights again and see the top of the tree with more cutout birds there as well.

Intriguing in its artificiality, this image displays three distinct levels of awareness which, along with the triangular, Christmas-tree shape suggest the trinity and underscore its spiritual meaning. The image also poses a variety of unsettling questions: Is the tree of my spiritual life really as phony, weak or flimsy as a stage prop? How is my perspective limited or compartmentalized? Am I failing to *raise my sights* enough for authentic (natural and rooted) spiritual growth?

This dream also contains an invitation: What else might I discover, if I were to recast this dream, through active imagination or creative expression, as a living tree with living birds?

In addition to the cranes and other water birds of the Gulf Coast, we share our landscape with the common, clamorous grackle, with its slender brown females and larger, eye-catching, gleaming black males. The grackle appeared to an anonymous dreamer just as he prepared to retire from a high-stress, high-profile career:

Grackles Nesting
Anonymous

I have been at a party or event. I go for a walk behind the building. As I turn to head back to the event, I notice a male grackle sitting on a nest in a hedge bush. The bird sits calmly as I look at it. I go to get my daughter so she can see. Then I notice there is an identical nest and bird in every third bush along the hedge.

In his processing, the dreamer recognized that the changes that would result from his impending retirement were this dream's core concern. Medical issues that had recently arisen seemed to be worsening under the stress of his job and were impacting his vision of the future. "At times I'm very concerned about my health and ability to continue functioning as I have in the past," he wrote in his journal. "I want to be sure my wife and I have a good quality of life upon retirement, but most of all I want to survive to enjoy it."

In this dream, leaving a public event (his workplace), the dreamer is drawn to the backyard – a deeper, private place where he might "explore, slowly and perceptively, changes in my life to learn more about myself." He finds new awareness in the bushes, or "in the shadows," and resonates with issues of dependence and independence that may be signified by nesting birds. Worth noting: the male grackle typically does not sit on a nest or incubate the eggs, making this dream even more emphatic in its meaning.

As an avid genealogy researcher, the dreamer sees a strong connection with his roots as well as a deep desire to tend his family in the present and the future. Familial implications of both the backyard and the nest are heightened by his intention to bring his daughter outside to see the nests, perhaps to help her learn more about family relationships and responsibilities.

Acknowledging his anxiety about retirement, he welcomed the grackle, which his research showed may appear when a person has been putting off dealing with significant emotions. He saw the nest as "the protective place that shields my spiritual nature" and a place to help him maintain control and increase his sense of security. Since birds themselves often represent the soul (both the dark and enlightened aspects), the grackle (among the blackest of birds) suggests the unknown, perhaps neglected, shadowy side of himself. As a Christian, the dreamer was particularly intrigued by the trinitarian placement of the birds and their nests in a distinct, every-third-bush pattern.

The dreamer engaged his grackle with the Magic Questions[1] developed by Robert Hoss. Taking the perspective of the bird, he wrote: "I am a male grackle. In the past, I have been quite showy, in the spotlight, but now I have retreated to my nest to nurture myself and mine. I am keeping a watchful eye for what is going on around me in case I need to fly. My purpose is to guard the nest and take care of what is inside it. I like my nest. It is well built and well situated. I have others around me who are similarly situated so I am not in this alone. I can fly if things get dangerous or it gets too risky. But I don't like being so fragile. It wouldn't take much to do me in. I could easily be killed or hurt. What I want most is for me and my nest to be safe."

As the dreamer has settled into retirement, meeting the challenges and opportunities of an active family, he continues to live out the messages of his grackle dream, tending his nest and depending upon his faith for his ultimate security.

Dreamer Becky O. has encountered various bird species in her dreams. First, we'll look at her peacock dream, then a series of snowy owl dreams, followed by a single dream of colorful birds. Together they illustrate the arc of her inner journey over a particularly challenging time in her life.

After becoming a spiritual director, Becky remained affiliated for many years with the retreat and spirituality center where she was trained. Peacocks, owned by a neighborhood resident, often sojourned in the sacred setting, delighting the sisters and retreatants alike with their beautiful, sometimes raucous, presence. What creature wouldn't want to gravitate to such a green and Godly space?

Here's how the peacocks manifested for Becky one night:

The Cenacle Peacocks
Becky O.

I am sitting on my twin bed in the Cenacle dorm surrounded by peacocks – males, females and three babies. Hearing a friend outside my door, I call, "Come quickly, Linda! God didn't know how to tell me how much he loved me, so he sent the animals!" I laugh and ruffle the heads and necks of the peacock babies.

Becky's spirituality often brims over with gladness and her dreams reflect this through laughter and enthusiastic engagement with the images and action. This lovely numinous dream has an obvious level of interpretation with its familiar setting and featured birds. Yet its simplicity is profound. As Becky engages physically, emotionally and spiritually with the feathered messengers, even ruffling the heads and necks of the trinity of babies, she happily receives the new wisdom they've come to impart. The glorious beauty of the peacock manifests in a rich context of masculine, feminine and new birth.

The following year, Becky encountered her soul guide in the form of the snowy owl, who entered her consciousness in this way:

Snowy Owl Dream #1
Becky O.

I am standing on my back porch looking out across our land, past the lake to the trees and the horizon. The wind begins to blow briskly from the south. White cartoon-like lines appear, swirling, curling and flowing, making the wind visible. I stand still in wonder. Then a snowy owl, also outlined in cartoon-like white lines, flies in on the wind. He hovers in front of me, wings outstretched, and says, "Wake up before you're dead!"

This dream's cartoon-like quality may suggest distancing as if the dreamer is not quite ready to accept the reality of what is coming into consciousness. Or the lines may be further defining the verbal message that can hardly be ignored. On awakening, Becky immediately recalled Antony DeMello's famous admonition to would-be spiritual seekers: "Wake up before you die!"

This initial appearance of her snowy owl was a literal wake-up call for Becky. While acknowledging her owl as a spiritual harbinger, she also took the dream's warning into waking life, applying it to her physical wellbeing, looking after her health and losing some extra pounds in the months that followed.

The owl made its second appearance two years later:

Snowy Owl Dream #2
Becky O.

I am at home with my whole family – a big gathering of loving people. The house is on top of a rise that gently slopes down towards a river. On either side of the treeless slope are forests of pine trees. Looking out the large windows in the back, I see something far away in the pale blue sky. I quickly run out onto the deck and I see it's a large white bird, slowly flapping its wings, heading my way. I run into the house and invite others to come and see.

A male presence with dark hair comes outside with me. We walk out on the deck then down the steps to the clearing that leads to the river. The bird is HUGE and is locking eyes with me. Clarity comes and I realize that it's a snowy white owl with a moon face! Steadily it flies straight toward me, lowering its altitude. Concerned it will hit me, I fall backward onto the hillside. But the white owl glides gently to a landing beside me and, without much ado, lies on its back to my left so we are side by side, looking at the sky. The owl, as large as I am, snuggles into the dirt closer to me. In a gentle gesture, it covers my lower body with its wing. It's an overwhelmingly joyful and lovely experience.

The male presence picks up a soiled cloth sheet used in yard work and laughingly teases us by throwing it over our bodies. We playfully toss it off and all three of us laugh. Then the giant white owl and I lie back in the dirt on our backs, happily connected, looking up at the light blue sky.

❣

Although Becky awoke from this dream smiling and amazed, this dream had a haunting effect ... for good reason. "I think the male presence was my dad, who died when I was 19," she said. "We'd spent lots of time outside together, admiring God's good creations. And he and I had used an old bedsheet to haul pine needles to the ditch to burn."

In her dream, Becky feels reassured on the hillside in the dirt (the gritty reality of earthly life), in companionship with the male presence (not only her earthly father, but also God the Father and/or Jesus), and the snowy owl (Spirit). The highest energy in this scene comes as the owl places its wing over her lower abdomen with the implication that something needs attention. In examination, it is clear that this dream presages a need for healing.

Only a few months after this dream, troubling symptoms led Becky to doctors who diagnosed a particularly aggressive form of uterine cancer. At this point, she was living out a personal commitment to companion her aging, widowed mother through her final year as her health declined and she required hospitalizations and increasing care. This loyalty led to Becky's decision not to tell anyone beyond her husband about her illness so she could protect her mother from concern for her.

So Becky continued caregiving and enjoying every opportunity for closeness that life offered her and her mother. Shortly before her cancer surgery and follow-up radiation, Becky was visited once again by her snowy owl:

Snowy Owl Dream #3
Becky O.

I am in a room, facing a large plate glass window that overlooks a beautiful mountain and valley. I'm in deep conversation with an unknown person when my attention is captured by a snowy owl sitting atop a tall pine tree in the distance. I am determined to hold presence with the person, but I cannot resist the thought of taking a picture of the owl. Slowly I ease my left hand into my pocket to get my smartphone while keeping eye contact with the person.

I furtively raise the phone to snap the picture. Then I notice that the scene is perfectly centered inside a gold circle. I gasp. As I move my thumb to take the picture the owl flies away. I continue to hold presence with the person but silently sigh at my loss. When the conversation ends, I quickly check my photos. The first one shows the treetop and the snowy owl, perfectly centered in the gold circle. It's simply beautiful and I smile in wonder.

Since Becky is a deeply contemplative spiritual director who trains others for this ministry, there's great tension in her dedication to holding presence with another while being compelled to attend to her owl. We can recognize the humorous impossibility of taking a smartphone photo without being noticed as a bizarre bit of dream logic. Yet knowing as we do about Becky's illness and her end-of-life journey with her mother, we can feel the poignancy of this inner conflict. Although the owl flies away as she prepares to take the picture, nevertheless, she captures a beautiful image.

The snowy owl's reappearance, even at a far distance, acknowledges Becky's deep recognition of her guide animal's presence. While the owl reminds her of its watchful care and ongoing wisdom, the gold mandala, a focus tool encircling the Self, preserves the photo for her to treasure during the time when much of her energy is outwardly focused before life allows her to turn inward to attend to her deeper Self.

Amid her snowy owl encounters, Becky had another dream in which she and her mother are together in the presence of birds:

The Caged Birds
Becky O.

Mother and I are eating in a lovely, bright restaurant with a high pinnacled ceiling. In the middle of the room hang birdcages of all sizes, with brightly colored birds of all sizes. As we chat, we hear ladies at the other table ooohing and aaahing, then a bit of muffled squealing. We look up and see that one of the birds has escaped and is fluttering in the tallest part of the high ceiling.

As I gaze up, the big, colorful, orange-green-yellow bird catches my eye. I lift my left hand, and she swoops down and lands lightly on my forearm. All the ladies are relieved, and Mother and I stand up to make our way to the open birdcage. We continue chatting as we walk, and the bird grows heavier and heavier. By the time we reach the open cage, I'm using both arms and hands to support the bird's weight and I'm unable to open the cage door wide enough for the bird to enter. Mother continues to talk, unaware I need her to help with the cage door. I continue to be present to her while I struggle with the weight of the beautiful bird.

Eventually, Mother notices what is required. We both laugh at her delayed realization and, as she opens the door wider, the bird flies in. As we close the door, we laugh about the importance of our shared stories. The ladies who have been watching return to their meals and Mother and I return to our table, still talking!

In this dream, the caged bird image is powerful – no small parakeet here but a multi-colored giant that Becky and her mother together return to its cage. Notice that, in approaching the cage, the bird becomes such an increasing weight that Becky needs the assistance of her internal mother energy to re-confine her vibrant energy.

Communication between mother and daughter takes center stage with the main thing being their "shared stories." Feminine energy abounds in this place of nourishment, with other parts of Becky's personality surrounding her and her mother. The colorful birds suggest a breadth of spiritual possibilities, all beautifully contained in a treasured way in a variety of cages.

As in the previous snowy owl dream, Becky's decision to be present to another means a tradeoff of her ability to "fly free." These dreams reflect in a tender way the life choices she was making – placing her own inner needs (instincts) on hold to prioritize love for her mother. Yet we, along with the dreamer, can feel confident that there will come a time to re-friend her snowy owl and to release her colorful bird to soar free.

Sometime after her mother's passing, Becky shared the following reflection: "I'm beginning to see that the big, colorful caged bird was the holy in the relationship between Mother and me. It sought me out (eye contact and landing on her arm), but Mother and I weren't yet ready for that holy shift in our relationship. So we put the bird back into its cage so we could continue our comfortable one-on-one conversation about our life adventures. The last week Mother was alive I felt that my bird was free as Mother and I experienced sacred encounters with angels, witnessed the Holy Spirit entering her, and shared a deep intimate invitation to trust as she was surrounded by eternal light and love."

Pause

In what forms, times and places have dream birds come to you? What invitation or assurance has your dream bird conveyed?

Snakes: Primitive Power

"Again and again ... the question comes up, "What are rattlesnakes good for?"
As if nothing that does not obviously make for the
benefit of man had any right to exist,
as if our ways were God's ways.... Anyhow, they are
all, head and tail, good for themselves,
and we need not begrudge them their share of life.

John Muir

The fantastic online article, accompanied by photos, seemed so improbable that I laughed aloud. A young woman who'd been sleeping in a nightly embrace with her full-grown python took it to the vet, concerned because her pet had stopped eating. After examining the healthy reptile, the veterinarian concluded that it had ceased eating in order to prepare its stomach for an especially big meal. Guess who was going to be dinner?[2]

A snake is a snake is a snake after all.

It's relatively easy for dreamers to think of naming, claiming and personally relating with a dream dog, horse, cat or bird. But the snake? Not so readily welcomed at first. Reptiles embody such ancient, elemental energy that a snake's appearance may call the dreamer to a level of pluck not required for other creatures. What is this primitive energy offering? What wisdom is it bringing forward? Although snake dreams may not be our favorites, they *always* warrant our attention.

Here is the first of my own two memorable snake dreams:

Rattlesnakes

A man is holding a long, pouch-like snakeskin. Smiling, he says, "Look!" He upends the snakeskin and a big rattlesnake falls out. Then I realize that it's only a baby because it hurries over to its mother, who is a HUGE rattler. *The mother's head is about a foot long and her body is proportional in size. The baby rushes up to her, smiling it seems, and burrows under the mother snake as she raises her coils to embrace it. It's a joyful reunion and I'm amazed to witness such obvious affection in snakes.*

This crazily brilliant little dream insisted I draw it, which I did in my amateur way, using colored pencils on a ruled page in my journal to create my snake mandala. I smiled in wonder the whole while, knowing these excellent snakes came to me with multiple levels of meaning, speaking through their size and power as well as dual-gender references.

The baby snake, sizable in its own right, is introduced by a cheerful masculine figure in an unmistakable phallic display, spilling the snake from a long snakeskin pouch. Then I see the massive mandala of the coiled mother snake, an image of the divine feminine, the great mother, embracing her baby. I'm astounded by this pulsating, larger-than-life presence.

While I hear no sound in the dream except the man's words, my soul feels the implicit energy of rattlesnake. I sense a shaman in a shuffling background dance, hear a *rattle-rattle-rattle* tugging at me. *"Pay attention! There's more here than you can absorb at a cognitive level. Much more than you can comprehend now."*

I know I have met the ancient serpent archetype. Simultaneously earthy and ethereal, heartwarming and haunting, these snakes and this dream continue to resonate in my life.

Flying home from a dream conference with Emma Adeline, I shifted from debriefing our wonderful experiences and began talking about animal dreams. She responded with mild interest, adding that she didn't consider herself "an animal person," and she *definitely*

wasn't a fan of reptiles … even though she'd recently had *another* dream about snakes.

Here is Emma Adeline's journey with the snake.

"Typically when things are scary or aggressive, I shut down," she said. "But the Dream Maker knew how to work with me and to meet me where I was." From today's vantage point, after several years of deepening dream study, she said her series began with "safe snake dreams" and gradually evolved into more dynamic relational interaction. "First, I simply hold and look at the snake, then I become aware of how the snake can bring healing and wholeness. Then I intentionally look at my own organic stuff, aware that as I change, those around me will see that and may also change. Finally, I experience affirmation and ongoing healing and, as I listen to my inner voice, I become more comfortable with my shadow." Along the way, she has discovered deep spiritual significance in the appearances of this creature.

With this summary as our preface, I invite you to walk with me through this illuminating snake dream series:

Introduction to the Snake
Emma Adeline R.

My husband and I are standing in our kitchen when I become aware of a small snake, about the size of a pencil, hidden among things on the cabinet. I see it and I watch, concerned, as it goes down the drain. That was not enough for me so I run hot water and say, "We'll make sure it will not come back."

Then I'm alone and the snake comes back, longer now. Somehow I take hold of it just behind the head and I try to decide how to kill it. I don't want it (the snake's essence) on my scissors or knife. So I just stand there, not afraid, but not completing the killing of the snake.

This dream came "like a gift" on Christmas Eve and Emma Adeline could not believe that she was so calm, actually holding her dream snake without panic or even fear. She noted that she didn't seek anyone else to handle the situation for her – a reflection of the conditions of her waking life in which she was responsible for her husband's Alzheimer care as well as her own ongoing recovery from cancer.

This initial snake appearance led her to consider personal associations. Recalling some distressing close encounters with snakes as a child, she was more keenly aware of the importance of the snake in Judeo-Christian tradition, citing a Biblical reference (Numbers 21:4-9) in which a bronze snake raised on a pole becomes a symbol of healing for those willing to look upon it. In the context of her faith, she accepted her first snake dream as the beginning of a more intentional look at her interior life.

A month later, snake reappeared:

Incarnation
Emma Adeline R.

I am standing just inside a doorway. I see two very thin pieces of what look like stiff, clear spaghetti on the floor. But then the ends (the heads and tails) begin to move although the middles remain stiff. Are these snakes? I'm concerned that they are in the house and I need to remove them.

To the right of the snakes is a children's bedroom with a baby bed. To the left is a large, open kitchen area. I stand and watch the snakes, anxious and pondering what to do. Then my daughter-in-law, mother of my twin grandchildren, comes from the children's room. She stops and hesitates.

I ask, "Do you see them?"

She says, "Yes." She remains calm.

At least I'm not the only one who sees the snakes. I am not crazy.

In processing this dream with her spiritual director, Emma Adeline saw the synergy of snakes and babies as presenting the ideas of gestation, birth and healing as processes. "The birth here is not just a physical birth, but a new awareness of my deep inner being and how it is being transformed."

The two snakes, possibly masculine and feminine, mirror the genders of her twin grandbabies and appear in the middle of the house, with rooms on both the left and the right suggesting connection or bridging. She added, "The fact that their bodies don't move, only the heads and tails, would seem to say that my head knowledge is dominant."

Emma Adeline believes that the lack of action in this dream is allowing her time to become accustomed to her snake appearances, "much the way animals themselves in nature often wait, very still, watching without doing anything." To her, the presence of her daughter-in-law, who represents some of her own traits, confirms that her whole being now sees and acknowledges the snake energy in the center of her home (life/psyche).

Her third snake dream came three years later.

Persistent Shadow
Emma Adeline R.

I am an adult, preparing for a "show and tell," like at grade school. I purposefully go to the store and purchase two snakes (not one but two!) and take them home. There I try to get one of them out of the baggie so that I can figure out how to handle it when I get to school and have to show it. The snakes are both in the same plastic baggie. The one I'm trying to get out is flat and the color of skin. The other one, round and dark in color, keeps coming out of the bag and I keep putting it back in. Both snakes move gently and curiously but not aggressively. I am cautious but not afraid. Throughout the dream, I'm aware of a presence with me over my left shoulder.

The qualities of opposites and the tension between conflict and cooperation coexist in this scene. "I feel these snakes represent my conscious and my unconscious or shadow self and I'm being very intentional about looking at all of it," Emma Adeline said. "But I seem to favor the skin-colored snake over the dark one." She notices that the pale, familiar (conscious) snake is flat and more passive, perhaps indicating that it has less substance and energy, consequently less to tell her, than the dark round (shadow/unconscious) snake that repeatedly tries to emerge. While she's proactive in engaging her snake energy (deliberately purchasing two of them) her favoritism in the dream suggests that she is still not quite ready to confront her baggage – shadow material she would rather keep confined in the unconscious (the baggie).

"I can only guess what the dream presence was," she said. "I'm hoping that it was God or a dream mentor, guiding me and my dream, and later the discernment of it."

A year passed before another snake visit:

Affirmation
Emma Adeline R.

I am outside, standing near a building talking with a female friend who notices a snake lying on the edge of the flowerbed. The snake is not moving or aggressive, just very still. It has a large head and a plump, round body. It looks very much like the dirt as if camouflaged. I'm not frightened and also not interested. I want to walk away from it. But my friend takes note of it and when we walk away from the house, around a large flowerbed, the snake follows, almost like a dog would, more like a domesticated animal than a wild one.

My friend reaches down to pick it up, but that is where I drew the line. I did not want to have anything to do with it.

I sense the nearby presence of a child – my grandson, who is a truth-teller.

In this fourth snake dream, Emma Adeline notes the strong structure of the building, the health and beauty of the flowerbed and the spirit-filled nature of the plump snake. This snake is the color of the earth, a foundational element in the psyche. Yet the dreamer tries to maintain her distance from this energy even though her friend attempts to interest her and even interact with it. Meanwhile, the friendly snake follows along in an endearingly domesticated way, inviting attention and engagement.

The sense of her grandson's presence is significant. This honest (truth-telling) youthful potential within lends credibility to the dream narrative and underscores the value of the scene that has just taken place. Emma Adeline said, "I see this dream as affirmation of my ongoing healing and transformation."

A year later her dream series continued the motif of change:

Becoming Comfortable with My Shadow
Emma Adeline R.

I am walking outdoors in an open landscape, but aware of only my immediate area. As I walk up a gentle incline, I hear myself thinking/saying: "I can stand under that ledge and I'll be safe." The ledge is high enough for me to stand beneath. Yet when a large brown snake tries to negotiate the ledge it is only eight or ten inches high.

I stand quietly and watch. The head and front part of the snake are suspended in the air and then it places its head on the lower area. But It seems to curl and misjudge the distance. So I put my left arm out to help it get its balance. The snake re-orients itself and crawls on its way.

While the snake's head was just over the ledge, half on and half off, I had a close-up view. It was a healthy, beautiful brown snake with a pattern of spots. It was as large as my arm and about four feet long. After it passed, I had the urge to hold it and put it up to my cheek and I wanted to show it to everyone.

In this dream, Emma Adeline once again equates the snake to her shadow, feeling strong confirmation about her relationship with it. Here she not only observes the snake but reaches out to help it regain its balance. She sees this as the need to balance intellect and instinctual energy and also conscious and unconscious material within herself. With her help, the snake is reoriented and able to move on its way. "Is this co-creation?" she wondered. Perhaps this is partly her deep recognition that the snake, as her shadow, is not infallible or totally self-sufficient. It too wishes to be recognized and included on the journey to wholeness and integration.

The setting of this dream (the ledge) and her protective action with the snake also reminded Emma Adeline of the story of Moses, who is told by God to stand in the cleft in a rock for safety as the glory of God passes by (Exodus 33:12-23). Seeing how her action reflected her growing sense of deep confidence and strength, she said, "Lately I am finding my own voice. Recently I have spoken up in places where I would usually have remained silent. Now I want to pay it forward by being in ministry with and for others."

From here, we see continuing progress in her perspective and deeper integration as two more recent dreams bring the snake right into the heart of her psyche and her life:

I Am with You Always
Emma Adeline R.

I am standing just inside the back door of my house and a snake comes toward me and into the house. The snake is small and young, but long. It seems scared and confused yet determined. I scream at Don, my husband, "I don't want a snake in my house. Why did you leave the door open so the snake could come in?" The snake darts under the washer and dryer. I'm still screaming at Don to get it out of the house. "How am I supposed to go to bed and rest knowing a snake is in my house?" The snake comes out from under the washer and goes down the hallway deeper into the house.

This snake's entry through the back door, "where family and friends enter," suggests familiarity and vulnerability. Notice that this snake knows where it belongs; it is Emma Adeline's energy and power and its rightful place is deep within her life and home. Significantly her husband Don was a carpenter and, during their long marriage, they constructed three houses together. "To me home means safety, family and possibilities."

She sees in this dream a deepening of trust and choices about her relationships with others and with God (here, her husband Don). "The snake seems to be God's spirit coming into me," she said, "and also to be my own spirit in the process of becoming. This dream reminds me that I am a new being now and that I will become more mature and wiser and more articulate in my relationships." She recognizes that she can indeed, even after strident resistance, welcome Spirit into her being and even sleep peacefully with this young, new learning deep within.

Her next snake dream increases the momentum in communication between conscious and unconscious:

Dream Maker Works in Secret
Emma Adeline R.

I am standing in my house, but it feels like I'm outside. Something or someone standing in an open field does something (unclear) and a long, healthy snake runs from it and heads directly for the house. The snake never slows down and then is in the house. I look at the window where the snake came in and there is a hole in the screen. I become aware that the snake has been coming in and going out before. I'm not scared, only observing, wondering what outside has scared the snake. It knows where to go to be safe.

"Standing simultaneously inside and outside is affirming the conflict in my waking life at this time," said Emma Adeline. "When the exterior difficulty cannot be immediately resolved, Dream Maker works in the depths of my being even, especially when I am too exhausted to continue." She recognizes that home (life/psyche) is the safe haven and the rightful place for the indwelling Spirit. "I know that 'The Lord will watch over your coming and going' (Psalm 121:7-8). And the Dream Maker takes me home to rest and pray until the challenges can be named and resolved."

To bring forth her snake energy more fully, Emma Adeline first answered the Magic Questions as the creature itself:

1. I am snake, a spiritual guide and mirror.
2. My purpose is to bring healing and wholeness.
3. I like pointing to deep understanding.
4. I dislike that the dreamer is either afraid of me or misunderstands my presence and purpose.
5. What I fear most is that I will be ignored or dismissed.
6. What I desire most is to be gentle and to offer wisdom when the dreamer is ready.
7. What I want to tell the dreamer is: listen to the indwelling Spirit. You are loved and whole. This will be an example to others.

Throughout her processing, Emma Adeline experienced the highest energy around the hole in the screen through which her snake comes and goes, so she also answered the Magic Questions from that perspective:

1. I am the hole in the screen, open from both directions to allow for insights.
2. My purpose is to allow movement as in the movement of Spirit in spiritual direction and in dreamwork.
3. I like being a hole because I am not dualistic. Others may choose to go through or not.
4. I dislike being a hole because I'm defined and limited by the material around me and I'm formed by the destruction of that

material. But I can unlearn unhelpful things about culture and religion that previously defined me, and I can seek out new trainings to expand my awareness.
5. What I fear most is that someone may *repair* me, closing me up.
6. I desire most to be of service to others and to be available when needed.
7. What I want to tell the dreamer: You are not defined by people with whom you disagree or by those who might try to pass through you ... only by how open, respectful and loving you are to your internal energies.

"God invites us and woos us," Emma Adeline said about her experience with this revealing series of dreams. Through her insights, we can witness the gradual opening of psyche to allow the ebb and flow of new power as her creature companion comes to entreat her recognition as she continues her journey of individuation.

♥

As I worked with Emma Adeline's dreams, the burgeoning energy of snake burst forth again into my own dream world in something quite different from my first snake encounter:

A Snake is Loose

A big snake is loose in my house and I am trying to kill it. My method seems to center on beating it with a stick. But the snake, a boa constrictor, keeps reappearing in yet another room. At one point I'm in the hall and I close my mother's bedroom door so it can't get in there.

Somehow through a long process, my feelings evolve from fear and desire to rid my house of this large creature to a compassionate attitude. So when I see the snake coiled in the corner of a room at the far end of the hall, I am relieved and grateful that I have not apparently hurt it with all of my efforts. I don't see any injuries and the snake seems to be looking at me. The snake's owner has been called and she will soon be here to get it. All will be well.

♥

Initially, this dream seems to say I've regressed. Unlike my *Rattlesnakes* dream of seven years earlier where my ego was a bemused observer, here I move to real, hands-on participation in the action ... distressing as it is. The Dream Maker knows I'm ready for a more personal encounter, although I heartily resist it at first. The snake's presence as a boa constrictor underscores my typical reluctance to loosen my constricting grip on my life, attitudes and perceptions.

In pursuing the snake deeper into my psyche, I make a critical shift from fear and rejection to compassion, even love. Along the way I pass the mother energy that connects this dream with *Rattlesnakes*, however, I feel that this divine feminine presence, which hardly needs my protection, is there to protect and reassure me on this pilgrimage deep into myself.

An unfinished aspect of this dream is that, even though I now relate to my snake with empathy, I have yet to integrate it (recognize the owner as myself). This recurring personal theme reminds me that my ego is not quite ready to claim my unfamiliar inner resources. In revisiting this dream, I might seek just such collaboration, following my snake to the depth of my psyche without weapons, meeting its gaze, befriending it, discovering how its powerful elemental energy is here to benefit me.

Pause

What creature energy is emerging unbidden in your dreams?
How might you carry new snake awareness
into your dreams and your waking life?

Sea Creatures: Deep Calls to Deep

There is the sea, vast and spacious,
Teeming with creatures beyond number –
Living things both large and small....
And the leviathan, which you formed to frolic there.

Psalm 104:25-26

The powerful imagery of water compels many dreamers into their depths. I remember my relief years ago when I recognized the metaphor of rising water in my recurring nightmare as a compelling invitation – that the boundary between water and not-water typically marks a threshold between conscious and unconscious. A frisson of recognition always accompanies my hearing or reading of "Deep calls to deep in the roar of your waterfalls. All your waves and breakers have swept over me." (Psalm 42:7) Yes! Water is so essential to life that its potential meanings in our dreams are virtually unlimited, spanning psychospiritual and physiological realms. Even more wondrous dimensions unfold when sea creatures appear.

Over the years my journey has been nourished by inspiration flowing from many directions and many dreamers who've preceded me. Two dream-writers worth special mention are Tallulah Lyons whose numinous encounter with the *Great Golden Fish* is featured in and on the cover of her book *Dream Prayers*[1], and Katherine Metcalf Nelson whose *Night Fishing: A Woman's Dream Journal*[2] comprises a stunning visual feast of dream art.

In this chapter, we loosely follow the pattern set for Part I, with fish being the sixth of Van De Castle's most common dream creatures. Beginning with a single fish dream of my own, we'll then move on to other dreamers' marvelous creatures of the deep.

Fish Out of Water

I'm in the women's restroom/dressing room near a beach. I'm wearing a swimsuit with a beach towel wrapped around me. I see a large fish that someone has placed in one of the sinks. It lies there in the empty sink, looking at me helplessly. It seems intelligent and connective. I run water to splash over it to make it more comfortable.

I hurry outside to see where I can take the fish to get it safely back into the water. Immediately left of the building is a beach where I can reach water deep enough to release the fish safely. I plan to carry it wrapped in my beach towel even though I will be exposing myself more than I like with just my swimsuit on.

I return to the restroom but, to my dismay, I find a young mother – a short, sturdy woman with reddish-blonde hair – and her three boys. She is holding the fish. It's clear that they had found the fish, put it there and consider it a plaything. They plan to keep it.

I tell them that I was going to take the fish back to the water because that was its home, hoping they will want it to be healthy and to live. But she is impassive, not rude, but not at all interested in my concerns. I feel very badly about this.

Long after I awakened, a sad, helpless feeling lingered. At first glance, this dream appears a call to better self-care (the suffering fish) or greater awareness of my psyche's interface with the external world. My fragmentation is evident. The high-energy (reddish-haired), no-nonsense (short and study) mothering part of me seems intensely focused on her agenda and her family – so much so that she appears oblivious to the needs or desires of others (the fish itself and me, the fish's would-be rescuer). She also draws my attention to the part of me that sometimes lacks awareness and sensitivity of others. Yet the three boys (youthful energy) plus their mother create four, the number of completion. Might there be something positive taking place with her claiming the fish, a symbol of spirituality?

This dream also points to other qualities I'd rather not face within myself. How in my waking life am I feeling out of place (like a fish out of water)? Where am I not fitting in? Always self-conscious about my physical appearance, I've never worn a swimsuit with confidence, so it follows that my dream ego wishes to remain wrapped up in a beach towel (avoiding exposure and vulnerability).

The bathroom, a place of cleansing, also provides the water for my baptism of the fish (a holy part of me) and our all-important, soul-connecting eye contact. Leaving that moment of divine communion, I move outside and leftward, toward intuition, with a strong desire to help.

But knowing that dreams have many layers of meaning, I also wonder if I'm not quite spiritually ready for that fine fish. A stronger, more confident part of me has assumed ownership, and while my judgmental ego presumes that she considers the fish a plaything, maybe that isn't the entire truth. Maybe this foursome, the mother and her three boys, are meant to hold and embrace that fish until I am fully ready for its message.

So, for now, I reluctantly leave the fish with them and allow this dream to rest in my journal, as a reminder that I have so much yet to learn.

When Becky O. and her husband built their retirement home in central Texas, they dedicated space on their acreage for a backyard labyrinth and a private lake. In Becky's dreams this lake has swelled up on several occasions to become a backyard sea and she has been ready.

In this first dream, she received a message of comfort shortly after the passing of a friend:

The Dolphin and the Dog
Becky O.

I am in my home with its big windows across the back. The glass back doors, however, look curiously like the doors to the hospital area where my friend Nancy's body is being kept until her organs can be harvested. Then I see that a calm, deep blue sea has risen amazingly to the middle of the doors. I see no field or trees, just a cloudless blue sky meeting the blue sea. I feel no fear or concern, just curiosity.

Then a creature comes towards me – a dolphin swimming on top of the water, smiling. By its side swims a black lab, also smiling. They come right up to the back doors which open slightly although no water rushes in. Both the dolphin and the dog lift their smiling faces for me to rub. I laugh, amazed.

Becky explained that at the time of another friend's passing, she had asked for and received a consoling response from her after she died. So on the day preceding this dream, before leaving the hospital, knowing her friend was near death, "I offered Nancy the invitation to let me know when she was surrounded by eternal light and love. This dream was a blessed ending to a sad day."

As Becky welcomes the dolphin messenger from the deep, it comes to her accompanied by a dog similar to her own beloved Labrador retriever, Jack. The dream presents a touching juxtaposition of two instincts – the familiarity of the loyal canine companion and the sociable nature of the dolphin, a creature who has long exhibited a special affinity for humans.

In this dream, Becky's psyche finds a uniquely compelling metaphor incorporating the lake that exists literally in her own backyard.

A year later, she was visited once more by an unexpected marine creature:

The Whale and the Guppy
Becky O.

I am passing the big window at the back of our home when I see the water in the lake moving. Looking closer, I see a dark hump rise and fall, but it's far too big to be a dolphin. I stand still, watching. Then I have clarity and squeal, "It's a whale! In our lake! I've always wanted a whale!"

As I rush towards the door, I notice a fishbowl on a table by the back door. I gasp as I see that the black guppy has grown until it takes up the whole bowl! His big eyes are pressed against the inside of the bowl. I gently lift the guppy out and start for the door.

A dark-skinned woman helper and her two children come in the door. I'm excited and announce the arrival of the whale. She casually says they have already seen it and goes on about her work. I continue out the door, excitedly carrying the big guppy, and now the water has expanded up from up the lake and is lapping around my feet. I let the guppy down gently into the water and marvel at the beauty of the whale.

My husband Richard is just arriving home, and I wave to him.

What a wonderful awakening dream. In Jungian-speak, the black whale, the black guppy and the black woman helper all represent the unconscious realm where the ego can begin the first stage of transformation. Notice that Becky's unknown helper already knows of the enormous untapped energy in the whale, and she even carries new potential herself as represented by her children.

Becky has always wanted this *whale* of a possibility, this great new awareness, but wasn't able to see it before. Now both the window and the over-sized eyes of the giant guppy highlight new clarity of vision and a new perspective. Contrast appears in the two children and in the tension between the great and the small – the whale which has come up from the depths and the once tiny guppy who has now grown to startling dimensions and potential and is ready to move into the deep.

The time is right, this dream suggests. The dreamer can now identify what a deeper part of herself had already seen. What great energy is already swimming free within? And what energy constrained in a small bowl has been growing until it virtually cries out to be set free? How will these great and small creatures come together in the lake of her unconscious?

"I am well grounded in this revelatory dream," Becky noted, "standing on the ground as the water rises and laps around my feet." She is also wholly within her feminine self, merely waving to acknowledge her masculine energy (projected onto her husband) as he arrives home to this remarkable scene. Significantly, at the time of this dream, Becky was discerning a call to a further level of training in her spiritual direction ministry, which she subsequently stepped into with great excitement.

Five years after this dream, several months after her mother's passing (see her dreams in the *Birds* chapter), Becky received a startling awareness linking this dream to her recent loss. "The beautiful black whale in our lake represents God, and I always want *more* God. The lake water rising to greet me as I exit our home is Spirit moving closer. And the guppy? Perhaps this is Mother, who has outgrown her earthly home. When I was with her during her last hours, she whispered, 'I see the Holy Spirit coming into me.' My commitment to her was to gently release her into eternal light and love. It seems I did just that."

Becky's new sense of this resonant dream was further highlighted by a poignant new awareness about the helper: "Mother's favorite caregiver was a wise Christian black woman who knew Spirit well. She escorted my sister and me (like the two children in the dream) down the hall as Mother's body was taken away."

Rest with this for a moment.

Dreamer Tiffany H. had a long journey with her animal guide before it manifested in her dream world. When she was twelve years old, the misdiagnosis of a ruptured appendix led to a month of suffering before major surgery finally put her on the way toward recovery. Throughout her illness and extended recuperation, she remembers her mother's loving care and her repeated watching of the movie that was to become a beacon for her life: *Free Willy*[3]. This was Tiffany's first encounter with orcas, popularly known as killer whales.

"Watching *Free Willy* was life-altering for me," she said. Her illness was frightening because no one could understand it or experience it with her. "I didn't feel prepared to handle all of that in my body and my spirit and I saw the fear of everyone around me." She saw her predicament of being trapped in an unwell body mirrored in the movie orca's suffering at its loss of freedom, and she was always heartened by the climactic scene of Willy jumping over a jetty to regain his freedom.

Although she recovered from her early illness, Tiffany was diagnosed with a chronic heart condition during college, so her health has remained a central concern for her since then. Meanwhile, she and orca have remained soul companions through dreams, visions and synchronicities that began in her twenties and have continued for more than fifteen years.

This shared journey has two dimensions, she explained: "One is the captured orca like Willy, the victim, the wounded, sick, trapped one, circling in the tank. The other version is the free, intuitive, wild animal which has a very different energy. The narrative of 'I can't' has been powerful in my illness. Sometimes I have felt like the wounded, sick one. But being a wounded one can border on glorification if allowed. In some dreams, I've seen the captive orca showing me that it's still there as a reminder, a warning. But wild blood still lives inside the orca in a tank just like wild blood is still in my bones."

Tiffany's experiences in waking life and in the dream world, with orca as her guide, reveal keen sensitivities and a poetic soul.

The following dream has come to her in various forms over several years. Here is its essence:

Awakening
Tiffany H.

I awaken to the ocean at dusk and see a rocky island in the distance. I am swept under waters that color and dance like the northern lights. I'm held by magic and the dance between light and darkness and depth of color. A great orca approaches and I am swallowed whole. I have no sensation except one of being held. In a seeming time warp, the moment ends, and I am spit out back into the calm water.

The sun is rising as I surface and raise my head to breathe the air and I realize I am human, not orca. The sunlight on my skin as I float feels like new medicine. I can smell deep forest smells from the shore, and it calls to a new place in me, a new home, a new experience. I wait.

Then I see an indigenous woman on the shore. Her back is to me and the ocean as she sits cross-legged before a fire, facing the forest. The hum of her presence is all essence and I feel as if our bodies are merged. She is crowned with white, gray, dark brown and black braids and skin that tells the story of both life and magic.

The sun begins to set, and I notice two glowing beings full of life, love and happiness on shore. They are human in all the humble simplicity of flesh but holy. They have come from the mountain trail, out of the forest trees, down from the village. I see them as Eric and Kai. Their eyes hold an invitation to me to come and walk the earth. They welcome me fully and wholly as I rise out of the ocean and take first steps toward them.

As the water drips down my face and legs, I turn to see a family of orcas adorned with malas in the distance. As the sun sets, they swim away toward the rock islands out in the depths. There's no breaking of bond, but an invitation to me to return as needed. Now I choose to walk on the earth. I am embraced by Eric and Kai as Medicine Woman plays her tune and dances her dance.

♥

Following the birth of her son and the replacement of her pacemaker, Tiffany had entered a period of deep psychic and physiological conflict. She felt herself shrinking and her body shutting down. Longing not to be ill, she wasn't yet ready or able to envision good health. Reflecting upon her illnesses and their ramifications, she said, "For years I've been cut off from the life that God has for me. And I've had to surrender to the deepest place inside of me, to get out of the idea of being a powerless victim."

Around the time she first experienced her *Awakening* dream, she made the conscious choice to embrace life and to intentionally move into the physical and deep inner healing she knew she would need to survive. "My journey has been a long one of moving into connection and full expression." Hers is truly a death and resurrection story. She senses in this dream echoes of her Christian upbringing. The rocky island and water remind her of Jesus meeting the invalid man who'd been lying by the pool of Bethesda for many years. "Do you want to get well?" Jesus asks. (John 5:6) This question has resonated deeply for Tiffany through much of her life.

The powerful orcas emphasize Tiffany's special relationship with water. As a youthful swimmer, she could stay underwater longer than anyone else on her swim team – which has undoubtedly helped her recognize and welcome her powerful orca energy. It also makes her specially tuned to the breath of life and the fact that orcas, being mammals, may remain submerged for up to twelve minutes, but *must* surface to breathe, just as she must.

Water has another meaning for her as well. "Being underwater has always been a haven for me. There's no need to explain or make sense of things there – just float and be present, release to the deep." As a child in a very large family, she had adapted by learning not to express herself. "I would make myself as small as possible to make others happy," she said. "But in water, I could hide, go under to a deeper world, protected by the blanket of water that mutes all sound, slows time and brings the beating heart forward."

One mark of the great devotion between Tiffany, her husband Eric and their son Kai (whose name is the Hawaiian word for sea), is the malas, the prayer beads, they all wear. In her dream, the pod of orcas, with a baby in their midst, also wear malas, mirroring the sacred unity of family.

In this dream, her emergence from the water to see her husband and son on the shore affirmed Tiffany's growing commitment to showing up authentically and opening her heart to share life with others. "I felt them telling me there was no need to stay underwater but to come walk with them." She felt called to a new life, a new way of being in the world.

During this period of her recurring *Awakening* dreams, came another powerful call to transformation:

The Orca and the Wolf
Tiffany H.

I am looking at a mechanical orca – a manmade metal article, the kind of displaced carnival machine that one might feed a few quarters to make it open and close its mouth before you walk away. After a moment, its eyes begin to glow.

Suddenly lightning flashes in the sky and reveals a live orca staring at me. I am face to face with the orca on the surface of the water. I am aware and present in my body. I can see my arms and hands and water around me. I feel at ease, with rhythmic breathing, like when I'm nursing my son or meditating. It's as if the orca and I are in the same realm.

Then I'm aware of other creatures in the water around me. I sink below a blue whale as it eats plant life, and I float towards its mouth. Then the ocean current returns me, still beneath the water, to the orca. We are in the moonlight. Time seems to stop ... it is a heartbeat and breath moment. Then lightning strikes again, and the orca is gone.

Suddenly I'm on dry land, looking up at a wolf on the mountainside. It stands on the edge of the cliff in all its wonder and mystery in the moonlight. The wolf howls, waits, basks in the moonlight. Our hearts beat together. The wolf bows toward me. Then it turns and runs into the woods behind it, in wild belonging, but with a calling and a promise.

I stand, wide-eyed, breathing rhythmically, fully present and fully alive. I can feel my body and my breath. I am made up of stars, with the power and wonder of the cosmos inside my body.

In this dream, Tiffany sees the mechanical orca's eyes as a window to the soul, yet this image also reminds her of a movie scene from her childhood with a mechanical guru in a turban inside a palm-reading, future-telling machine. While she was always interested in the mystical realm, her family discouraged those inclinations, so the mechanical man's glowing eyes became part of the off-limits, scary unknown.

With a shift in dream consciousness, she moves toward the more instinctive left and becomes aware of water. While the (real) orca remains on the surface, she sinks and is carried by the current. As a child, Tiffany was terrified by the thought of being in the water near a large creature or a ship, making this dream striking in its content and affect. Yet here she simply surrenders to the current, neither swimming nor fighting, but moving along where the dream takes her. The intense awareness of her own presence is significant. Historically, even when sick and in pain, she always felt more like an observer than an inhabitant of her own body. Here she is fully integrated as well as connected to the orca, "to the truest parts of myself and life."

With a scene change, Tiffany's attention moves from the water of the unconscious toward consciousness, toward land and new energy, the wolf. "It's possible," she said, "that the wolf isn't a new creature, but a new language of the orca. Because it's so fully present and also wild, it reminds me of how Christ is described as fully human and fully divine. I see the wolf connected to spirit."

Over several years of intense inner work, Tiffany has seen how she had habitually blocked out and silenced her own voice, the authentic expression of herself. "I've been deeply uncomfortable with a full expression of self and beauty." In reading Clarissa Pinkola Estés' *Women Who Run with the Wolves*[4], she is coming to know the woman within herself who will no longer be held captive by old negative ways of seeing and being in the world. "I have lived underwater and been comfortable there. Now I think that someday I can run and leap and howl on the earth. A sacred wild is calling."

Today Tiffany arises before dawn each morning to walk barefoot in a beautiful green space near her home and, at the end of her walk, she stops to meditate near the statue of a wolf pack. There one morning she was joined in her meditation by the orca, the wolf and an indigenous girl. "The three were sitting in a wooded setting, equally spaced and they broke sticks of agreement and burned them. When only one stick was left, the orca snapped the last stick in its mouth." She explained that this ritual with sticks of agreement frees a captive from an agreement made earlier in a time of weakness. After the orca snapped the last stick, she saw it enter water and swim away with its fin upright, not slumped to the side as is common among orcas in captivity.

For a time Tiffany wondered if orca had shape-shifted to wolf in her psyche or if both of these powerful creature archetypes would remain as companions on her journey. In answer, they have both appeared as she identified her seven chakra animals. She found orca residing in her third chakra, the solar plexus, helping her access her personal power and apply it in deliberate, effective ways. Wolf lives in her fifth chakra, the throat, empowering her self-expression and communication. In her crown chakra, she discovered medicine woman, a spiritual complement to her recent opening to the indigenous energy in her own family as she learns about her great-grandmother, who was a full-blooded Cherokee.

Tiffany continues to be visited by orcas in her dreams as they gently and persistently encourage her onward toward healing and wholeness. In a recent dream, she and two families of orcas watched as a massive ship sank, "being digested by the ocean." One orca group seemed foreign and mysterious, but the other pod of four orcas reflected the glow of a distant city. "The light shone on their wet skin as they beheld the scene of the great ship. This pod was adorned with malas and they swam off," she said.

As this great ship of her past (old self-perceptions, attitudes and ways of being in relationships) slip away like the Titanic to be "digested" in the great unconscious, Tiffany sees the great quaternity of completion in the pod of four orcas. Wearing her own mala symbol (they belong to her), the orcas turn away from the past to guide her toward the warmth, the light and the new life of the beckoning city.

Pause

What dream creature is swimming up to the threshold of your consciousness? How do your sea creatures, and water itself, speak life-giving words to you?

Bugs: The Many-Legged

> *too many creatures*
> *both insects and humans*
> *estimate their own value*
> *by the amount of minor irritation*
> *they are able to cause*
> *to greater personalities than themselves*
>
> Don Marquis

Growing up in the Pacific Northwest, I never noticed cockroaches. I suppose they were around somewhere, but I was so obsessively repelled by the pervasive slugs that I suppose I had no energy left for dreading insects. That all changed when I moved south with my enlistment in the Air Force and discovered that even spotless living quarters could be infested with creatures that emerged at every dark opportunity, intruding through the tiniest openings into my space, my world.

I suspect that the dearth of bug dream submissions for this book says less about the actual *quantity* of such dreams and more about dreamers' general unwillingness to spend time with them. After all, who wants to dream about, much less journal or process our encounters with shudder-worthy small creatures. We know, however, that an estimated ninety-plus percent of all animal life forms fall into the insect category … and that doesn't even cover the eight-legged arachnids. With all this creeping, darting, flying, swimming, swarming behaviors, there's little wonder that bugs appear to us at night.

What's bugging me now? is the classic question we might first ask ourselves when we awaken from such encounters. My dream journals reveal a number of these disturbing dreams and, while I would prefer to ignore them, I feel compelled to offer a couple of cockroach dreams:

The Giant Roach

I am outside alone by a concrete wall when I see a huge, foot-long roach-like bug. It's way too close to me. I call out, "Will somebody come kill this bug?" It prepares to fly and I'm afraid it will land on me – and it does! I'm trying to get it off me when I awake in alarm.

Around the time of this dream, my journal entries indicate over-involvement in so many spiritual activities that I was giving only brief attention to silence and solitude before rushing forward into worthy pursuits. I was overwhelmed by Richard Foster's oft-quoted "muchness and manyness"[1]. And I recognized this enormous roach, a palmetto bug, as the single representation of all the separate (self-imposed) small things that I felt were flying at me.

Only a few months later I received the following dream:

Roach Infestation

I'm preparing to move to a place where I know there are lots of roaches. I know they infest the walls and will be everywhere so that I'll need to turn on a light when I get up during the night to scare them into hiding. I know I will need to get a bed frame to lift the mattress off the floor. Then I realize I can buy lots of roach baits to attract them and keep them away from me as I bring them under control.

Curiously I don't actually see a single roach in this dream. It's all an intellectual awareness of the situation I will be in if I continue on the path I'm currently following.

In the case of roaches, shedding light on the matter simply pushes the problem scurrying back into the dark unconscious. So

Dream Animal Wisdom

merely turning on a light is a temporary fix at best. Ensuring that my mattress is raised from the floor and having roach bait traps to attract the creatures away from me may be useful steps, but even so, my troubles will still be there. What is bugging me indeed! The dream's final sentence tells me that whatever the annoyances or problems in my waking life, they will continue crawling around in my psyche until, unless, I take some truly effective steps to handle them.

I'm pleased to turn now to two other dreamers who have shared their bug dreams and the substantive insights they've received through their encounters.

First, we'll explore the dream of a spiritual director and relatively new dreamworker, Stacy Boyer. Stacy is a partner in a small-town business that specializes in needlework and quilting, along with on-site Bible classes. She and her friend and partner, Carol, are "like spiritual sisters," and their complementary gifts and talents support good teamwork in their business and ministry.

After several weeks of business closure due to the COVID-19 pandemic, Stacy found herself in sorrow and confusion. Besides her concern about the business and other aspects of her creativity, she was dealing with recent hurtful encounters at church, where she serves in leadership. Into this context she dreamed the following:

Two Bugs in Hand
Stacy Boyer

I'm in a large gathering of people in a dark, theater-like setting with padded chairs and a stage. I'm excited because I'm there to support Carol who is taking the stage to speak and teach. I'm also a bit anxious because I know this will be hard for her and I want her to do well.

Someone hands me a square black cloth like a washcloth with a ladybug and another winged insect with spindle-like legs on it. The ladybug stays still on its left half of the cloth. The other bug keeps moving around on the right side. I know I'm supposed to give them to Carol – they're essential to her doing a good job – but the program is starting and there's no way to get them to her through the crowd and without interrupting her talk. So I take a seat in the middle of the auditorium.

The spindle-legged bug keeps flitting around, crawling off the black washcloth and disappearing. Yet I'm aware of its presence even when I can't see it. It's wispy in nature and I worry I will lose or injure it. Finally, I give up and concentrate on the ladybug. It's a little larger than normal, bright red with three perfectly placed black spots on each wing. The ladybug never moves or shows signs of life, but I know she is alive.

❣

"The overall feeling in this dream is anxiety," Stacy said. "I'm drawn to the color and beauty of the ladybug, but the other bug is difficult to keep up with." When she gives up trying to keep track of the flighty bug and focuses on the ladybug, she feels a sense of resignation. She had intended to give both bugs away (to Carol) but one was better than nothing. "And the ladybug was easy to see, easy to contain, and beautiful to look at."

At first, Stacy resisted considering what the two little creatures signified but finally admitted in her journal: "These bugs represent parts of you. Consider both of them. Look closely!"

The Enneagram[2] provided one tool for examining her dream. "I'm a seven on the Enneagram," she said, "an enthusiast and encourager. And the spiritual gifts assessments I've taken over the years always show I have the gifts of encouragement and faith." These understandings have helped Stacy learn to communicate, at least to those close to her, about her hopes and her waking life dreams, and to be more aware of how to encourage others "without trying to escape the hard or painful places in life." Dealing with others beyond family and friends, however, has been much harder. During one period of journaling, she heard the question: "When have you felt squashed lately?" Her answer came quickly. In recent church meetings, she had felt completely discounted, "totally flattened and embarrassed."

Stacy admitted that during her life she has typically expended considerable energy attempting to present the part of herself the world considers valuable – the beautiful ladybug who's compliant, perfect (with symmetrical spots), knows the rules and stays within her space. "The ladybug is easy to love," said Stacy. "I can keep up with her and those I give her to will like what they hear and see."

Meanwhile, she said, "I've lived ashamed of my 'other bug' nature – the one that flits around, who finds joy in movement and goes beyond constraints (the border of the black cloth), exploring possibilities and out-of-the-box ideas. I don't often share that part of me with others because it's too much trouble to deal with. It's easier to keep it under wraps than to have others squash it." In the past, she said, "I've been hurt by others' responses – words like *irresponsible* and *Pollyanna* – and by having my ideas dismissed as over-the-top, crazy, impossible, overly optimistic."

One day following her spiritual reading about the value of individuals, she wrote in her journal: "Oh my! I often hide the other bug self because the world does not consider it valuable. Maybe I have come to a place that I don't value it either!" By over-emphasizing the more acceptable part of herself, she said, "I see that this way of living is keeping me bound by borders (like the ladybug). I'm alive but not moving."

She began to understand that her dream was offering an invitation toward integration and balance. The contrast between Stacy herself (Enneagram 7) and the part of her represented by the more meticulous, detail-oriented Carol (Enneagram 1) is mirrored in the two radically dissimilar but valuable insects.

In the dark theatre, the two bugs appear against a dark background (the black washcloth-like square) as the psyche invites Stacy into the darkness of the unconscious. The four-sided cloth is rich in symbolism – strength and stability – in addition to the Jungian understanding of the squaring of the circle (mandala) as an image of the Self and an archetype of wholeness. The position she takes in the center of the auditorium also indicates she is ready for this encounter with her deep Self.

A long interest in Biblical numbers has led Stacy to a strong association with seven as the number of completion. By extension, the number six means something is not quite finished, something is missing. So her ladybug, even with its symmetrical six dots, isn't quite complete in and of itself. "Six represents for me a time to wait and allow Spirit to work until six moves to seven in wholeness and completion." It is the stout little well-behaved ladybug with her six perfect spots, plus the other lithe and venturesome insect who together make the totality of Stacy.

Holding this dream, Stacy continues to honor it as a vital step in her journey of individuation. "Lord, what does it look like for both bugs to coexist, to come together so that I may become the person I'm designed to be?" Significantly, both of Stacy's dream creatures have wings, with which she can surely fly.

And now, the spider.

One cold, damp Seattle winter of my childhood my family lived in the daylight basement of the house we were building, awaiting spring to resume construction. There my mother created a warm home for us amidst the bare-stud walls and roughed-out rooms. Each night, although she feared spiders, Mother came into the darkened bedroom I shared with my older sister to bravely confront the spiders who, if left alone, would leave me with great welts from their bites by morning. It's one thing to know that Spider holds a respected place among archetypes, spirit guides and totem animals. It's quite another to welcome spiders when they creep into one's bed or one's dreams.

My own encounters with dream spiders began early in my dream journey and quickly showed me the complexities of this image in my psyche. For example: *I dream of two large spiders in webs at the side of my house and I don't want to destroy the webs or kill* the creatures but "I can't go down that side of the house" unless I do. Another dream: *A giant spider is missing one leg, but I have a magic wand and I wonder if I can restore her leg.* While my realistic dream spiders generated apprehension, the great cosmic spider put me in touch with greater (even magical) powers than I ever knew I possessed.

❣

Here is the richly detailed spider encounter of dreamwork consultant Amy Curran[3], who commonly removes arachnids from her house so they can go on about their lives outdoors:

Black Magic Spider
Amy Curran

I'm in my kitchen and I open the cupboard to the left of the oven. I reach up for a zip-locked, ridged, stand-up, milky-colored hard plastic bag – about 6 by 10 inches in size. I place it on the kitchen counter and open it to peer inside. What I see is a one-third-full bag of what looks like salt and pepper or maybe fine sand. When I start to zip it back up, a small, one-third inch black spider jumps out and lands on the side of the bag. This surprises me and I wonder what the spider was doing in the bag and if there are any others that I didn't see.

❣

In counseling with her clients, Amy encourages them to explore images and emotions, to tap into the felt sense of the dream and to keep the dream alive, inviting additional insights as understanding develops over time – all of which she applied in working with her own dream.

Amy carried her spider dream in her mind for several days. "When it landed on paper," she said, "I was still unaware of its significance."

Nevertheless, she knew that she would share this dream with her small group at an upcoming dream conference. Receiving the projections of group members on her dream, she resonated with many images and energies. Adding these to her emerging associations, she compiled the following connections and ideas.

Considering the implications of the dream setting, she said, "The kitchen is my domain, a place of nourishment. I love to cook and bake." The bag's placement to the left of the oven is referential to her left-handedness as well as a movement of the dream material into intuition and receptivity.

The bag itself is rich in meaning. "Do I 'zip it up' and avoid talking?" she asked herself. "Or do I open up to the surprise within?" While closed, the bag's milky surface obscures clarity about its contents so she can't see inside. The ridged stiffness, which allows the container to stand up on its own, also suggests an invitation for Amy to loosen up, to be more flexible, perhaps to open up and share what is within, which might not only be a gift to others but a surprise to herself.

Amy looked at the multiple numbers in the dream. The bag is only one-third full and the spider is one-third inch in size. "Perhaps I need to be more optimistic about my life," she said. "Maybe my life is only one-third full and I need to find the other two-thirds to make it whole." Considering the six-by-ten size of the bag, she multiplied the numbers. "When I reach age sixty in just a few years, I imagine I will have lived two-thirds of my life. It looks like I have a lot of work to do in a short time."

Applying the Magic Questions to the contents of the bag, Amy answered first as salt and pepper (the *spice of life* and *the salt of the earth*, a term for a good and honest person); and second, as fine sand (*the sands of time* and the passage of time in an hourglass).

1. I am the contents of the bag – salt and pepper or fine sand.
2. My purpose as salt and pepper is to provide added flavor and spice. As sand, my purpose is to provide a place for sea turtles to lay their eggs deep into my warm, protective layers.

3. What I like about being salt and pepper is that I am a gift of the sea (salt) and the land (pepper). As sand, I offer protection for the incubation of new life.
4. What I dislike about being salt and pepper is that sometimes I'm used together and other times separately. As sand, I dislike getting moved around and always changing shape.
5. What I fear as salt and pepper is that I will be mixed up and no one will use me. As sand, I fear I will get washed away with the waves and the tides.
6. What I desire as salt and pepper is that people will use and enjoy both of me. As sand, I desire to be fluid with the waves and tides of time.
7. What I would like to tell the dreamer as salt and pepper is: do not be afraid of mixing it up and adding some spice to life. As sand, I would like to tell the dreamer: I am always moving and shape-shifting but I will never go away.

Notice that it's not important to Amy to definitively identify the bag's contents as one or the other. The psyche provides both because each offers a different perspective for her life. Salt and pepper relate more directly to her ways of being in the world, while the sand takes her into a deeper realm and even links this dream to another of her powerful dream creatures – the sea turtle. (See *Spiritual Menagerie* chapter).

Looking at the creature itself, the jumping spider leaps out of the bag as if to say, *Here I am! Thanks for releasing me from the salty/sandy ocean of the unconscious. I have things to tell you.* "The spider itself was magic to me in the most positive sense!" Amy said. "What is jumping out at me in my life?" The jumping spider (scientific name, *Salticidae* – there's the word *salt* again) has excellent vision and is capable of crossing long gaps.

Here is how this little creature answered the Magic Questions:

1. I am the black spider.
2. My purpose is to spin webs and capture things.

3. What I like about being a black spider is that I can spin webs over and over again.
4. What I dislike about being a black spider is that I surprise people and they are fearful of me. (Amy has discovered in her consulting business that dreamwork can be disturbing to some people.)
5. What I fear about being a black spider is that I will get squished and not be set free or that my web will get destroyed and I will be unable to create it again. (Amy acknowledges a fear of failure and of her work being unrecognized.)
6. What I desire as a black spider is to be seen and appreciated as a weaver of webs (a dream weaver) with intricate designs, and for my strength, resilience, ability to catch things and to begin again.
7. What I would like to tell the dreamer is that the spider's job of weaving webs can teach you something. Nothing ever stays the same, so we must learn to change and adapt every day.

Amy resonates strongly to the spider archetype as weaver of the web of life, and to its eight legs signifying wholeness and infinity, the symbol of beginning over and over. Also, the spider is the sacred bringer of creativity and feminine energy and it raises questions of change and death and immortality, encouraging one to face one's darker self. "The Taoist perspective sees life as finite and believes that wishing to live beyond one's natural life span is not in the flow of nature," she said. She also notes that some spiders weave a web at night, and pull it apart in the morning, prepared to reweave it later that night.

Amy gathered many associations from arts and literature, including the Gary Wright song *Dream Weaver*; the children's classic tale *Charlotte's Web,* the nursery rhyme *Little Miss Muffet*. She also related to Spider Woman, a hero with super-human senses and bodily resistance to injury. She was exposed to radiation – as Amy was when she received radiation for breast cancer – and it was from this exposure that Spider Woman gained her superpowers. "She is not only able to fly but discharges bio-electrical energy from her hands."

Amy said that *Black Magic Spider* has invited her to a much deeper connection with Spirit. "We are not apart from the world in which we live, but rather a vital thread in the universal tapestry. Without our input, the tapestry will fray and eventually fall apart." In processing this dream she has used a variety of creative tools, turning her dream narrative into a poem and collaging with magazine images. "And I know that in my work with others and their dreams I can help them create something beautiful."

Today she continues to treasure this dream as a valuable part of her evolving self. "One thing I'm discovering through my experience with breast cancer is that time cannot wait for me to manifest my dreams! I believe that my spider dream was given to me to help make meaning of this message."

Pause

What unwanted dream creature have you been most avoiding?
How might you revisit your disturbing creatures
and invite them to reveal their messages?

Turtles: Ancient Ones

*One origin of the world story teaches
that the earth rests on the back of a giant turtle.
But what's beneath the turtle? you ask. A bigger turtle.
And under that? Well, an even bigger turtle.
And after that? Oh, stop asking!
It's turtles all the way down!*

An Oft-Embellished Ancient Myth

In my second year of dream-tending, my psyche announced: *All right. If you're really serious about this inner work, get ready to take a plunge.* A newborn turtle showed me the way:

Birth Day of the Sacred Turtle

The day after a celebration, a birthday party for me, I'm cleaning my kitchen. Other people, maybe lingering from last night, sit at the table. I'm wiping down the side of the refrigerator when I discover a small cocoon – no more than an inch long. It's like a mud dauber (wasp) nest with a hole in one end. As I prepare to remove it, a tiny creature begins to emerge. It's a baby turtle, beautiful, luminous and iridescent in color. Suddenly it's much larger, almost as big as my hand. I hold it gently but firmly in both hands and hurry outside to take it to the water.

I rush down the grassy expanse behind my house to the lagoon. To my right is the house of a friend where she and her large family are relaxing on her porch. I call out to tell them about finding the turtle and how I'm on my way to set it free. "I hope the little guy will know what to do," I say. They call out encouragement. When I near the water I see two turtles there so I feel hopeful. At the water's edge, I release the baby turtle and it immediately swims away to the right.

Then I am chest-deep in the water myself, fully dressed and with my glasses on. Many people are around me, also fully dressed. I see a tall, dark-haired man with a beard whom I remember from last night's celebration. He's still in his tux and wears his glasses, which reassures me that it's all right for me to be wearing mine. He smiles at me. I am preparing to submerge and swim and it all seems okay.

❦

Although I knew immediately that this was a Big Dream, I didn't understand at first that a profoundly important animal guide had appeared. When I told my daughter about the dream, she reminded me that turtles had been part of my life for years, triggering a rush-back of memories like the turtle pets of childhood and rediscovering the remnants of my long-ago turtle collection scattered around my house. My turquoise and silver turtle ring. Turtle trinket boxes. Turtle figurines. Turtle images on my office bulletin board. My daughter was right. I'd had an affinity for turtles long before I could have articulated why.

There may be no more apt animal companion for a personality type than the turtle for introverts. As a relatively self-contained, independent loner, I can withdraw into myself whenever I wish, and my shell offers protection against intrusions. Yet these easily spotted associations were merely the surface level of my connection with turtle. Clearly, this dream was calling me deeper.

Birth Day of the Sacred Turtle intrigued me with its setting – the morning after a milestone celebration in my life. For how long has this aspect of myself (the cocooned turtle) been waiting (kept on ice, so to speak, on the side of the refrigerator)? The location of the cocoon at my heart level suggests that I must be open to something other than a cool intellect to receive this numinous message. As I hurry outside, still oblivious to the turtle's arrival as *my* guide, I express my naïve concern to the neighbors as if the turtle might not know what to do once in the water. The turtle's immersion and direction to the right (also my direction when I enter the water) indicate new material coming to consciousness.

This dream was still fresh when I had the chance to present it in a dream animal workshop. My notes from that day still reverberate with the group's wisdom: the transformation inherent in the turtle's metamorphic birth from a cocoon, the salty, (amniotic) fluid of the lagoon signifying archetypal birth, my baptismal entry into the depths of my unconscious, and the focus on clear, new vision (the eyeglasses). All of these projected insights encouraged me to hold this dream in a continuing embrace. The dream's clear message about my birth into a new journey became a pivot point in my waking life as well.

Intuitively I began gathering turtles again, this time intentionally, with a clear purpose to bring my dream image forward in tangible ways. I drew pictures and collected figurines, including a hand-sized turtle carved from jasper that sits in front of my keyboard as I type these words.

After this dream, more than two years passed, during which I had successful treatment for breast cancer, then resumed an active life, both waking and dreaming. When turtle reappeared, I was heartened to know that my Big Dream hadn't been an anomaly, but indeed foreshadowed an ongoing relationship.

In this next dream I observe a church friend using turtles from my collection to convey a vital message:

Turtles on the Altar

I am indoors, seated several rows up on bleacher-like seats. At the ground level, Sue is arranging an altar on a table. Several women offer Sue items she can use. One gives her a green turtle box (like the one in my collection) and she places it among the other items. Then another woman gives her a turtle figurine I recognize as mine. It is palm-sized, shiny and green like the turtle box, but this one is a sculpted piece. Sue holds it, considering where to place it on the altar.

I'm surprised that others are freely giving my turtles away, yet I don't feel possessive about them. I realize this is all very important somehow. In a lucid moment, I understand the message of the turtle: wherever you are you are home because you carry your home with you. I awaken in surprise.

♥

This dream introduced some timely questions about the relationship between my turtle and my faith. How was I, a mainstream Protestant Christian, meant to hold my deepening commitment to dreamwork and my faith? What was I to do about my new turtle awareness? How was turtle given to me to use and experience in community, in relation to my church? This dream prompted me to see both my psychospiritual development and my faith fully embodied in Turtle, the most ancient of all reptiles, the creature who lives to astonishing ages, carrying its home along with it.

The setting for this dream is humbling. During the time of this dream, I was becoming deeply involved in spiritual direction and in leading retreats, workshops and classes on spiritual topics. While these activities all emerged from my enthusiasm for spiritual discovery, I heard this dream's caution not to set myself higher than others (up in the bleachers), but to become more grounded. "It's okay to have your head in the clouds, but keep your feet on the ground," a dear friend used to caution me. In contrast, the bleacher stairs remind me of Jacob's ladder, suggesting that I have ready access upward and downward, enabling me to connect all my spiritual and secular roles and responsibilities.

My friend Sue's presence is significant. Knowing her as a lifelong Christian and practical, down-to-earth woman, I ask myself how I might become more like her. It is the realistic Sue part of me who understands how and where to place my turtles on the altar in a meaningful way. My familiar green turtle box represents all of my past and experience while the turtle sculpted of solid green material tangibly represents all the hope, renewal and new growth I might now learn to bring into the world.

Turtles on the Altar became a profound metaphor for my journey. Sue and the other women show me the rightful place of my turtle in relationship to my faith. My study of dreams and the precious gift of this animal guide, are not meant merely to edify or entertain me. My dreams are given by the Dream Maker to inform, inspire and equip me to be increasingly useful in service to others in the world.

A year later, turtle returned in this improbable dream:

The Turtle and the Spider

I am outdoors at the corner of a brick building when I see a square spider web and a large spider. Then to my amazement, I see a hand-sized turtle caught in the web! I had no idea that a turtle could climb up so high or that a spider could capture a turtle. I'm preparing to free the turtle when it struggles from its cocoon-like entrapment and crawls away. It moves upward and to the left, around the corner of the building. I realize that the turtle must have been captured for its wisdom.

It was challenging to extricate my attention from the striking image of a square spiderweb because I instantly recognized my neat, overly structured sense of order. What's more, the web was attached to an unyielding, right-angled brick building (my way of life). My poor turtle didn't stand a chance! Over time, however, this dream began to reveal more. A new level of awareness opened up as I saw the web as the work of the great cosmic weaver and the square mandala, a symbol of Self.

What first seems like entrapment (a cocoon-like presentation similar to my first turtle appearance) may simply be an image to shake me from complacency. Once I acknowledge the situation and see there's something larger at work here, the spider energy releases its grip so that turtle may once again lead the way. Leaving my structured, orderly self behind, she disappears leftward into my more instinctual self.

In the months after this dream, my psyche followed turtle into a rich time of shapes, symbols and synchronicities. One day I drew a circular turtle mandala with a web design, complete with spider, on its shell. Another day in an airport bookstore, I found a Native American storybook for children showing turtle with the sign of the spider (a web-like pattern) on its shell. I began to understand turtle as carrying the web of my life and my home in its unique self. In a meditative dialog, turtle responded to me with these words: "Allow me to be woven into your life. I am both commentator and guide. I can lead you both deeper and higher in your journey."

My dream journal began to include waking visions and synchronicities – spotting red slider turtles at the park, rescuing a box turtle from the middle of the road on my way to church, and visioning a hand-sized empty turtle shell, its yellow-gold under-shell turned toward the sky.

Noticing that many of my turtle images and dreams carried the *hand-sized* descriptor, I considered what it might mean that turtle fits so neatly into my hand. Is turtle's life force flowing into me that I might absorb its energy for giving, serving, touching others?

Two months later I had a dream that shifted focus from my hands to my feet, raising the question of where I was heading in my life:

The Injured Tortoise

I'm in the upper story of a building, looking out a window onto a broad, paved intersection of streets. I see four giant tortoises. One appears to be injured with a lame left front foot as if it had been hit by a car. The other tortoises hover around it, as some animals do when a mate or companion is wounded. I'm surprised by their behavior and concerned for the injured one. Then three of the tortoises begin to move away to the left, and I see that one carries a baby tortoise on her back.

My journal contains a sketch of this image with notations about the four tortoises, their four legs (including the injured one), the four elements, directions, seasons, and the four possibilities offered by the intersection of streets. This dream also harkens back to the square spiderweb, the significance of the number four and the square mandala.

Notably, my tortoise quartet begins with wholeness, but four moves to three as the uninjured ones depart. What is fragmenting within me? What part of me is on troubled footing? Am I to tend the injured one? Or am I to follow the healthy tortoises as they take the fresh, new possibility (the baby) in a new direction?

This dream ushered in a tender cycle of life and death. Soon afterward I found a dead baby turtle in a parking lot; I dreamed of a dead, hand-sized turtle; then at the park, I watched in awe as a platter-sized red slider excavated a hole with her hind feet, laid her clutch of big rubbery white eggs, diligently covered them and plodded off toward the lake. During a nap that afternoon, I dreamed the mother turtle appeared outside my garage.

Without a doubt, turtle had claimed me.

Continuing my dream tasks, I copied all the turtle dreams from my chronological journals, making a separate notebook to honor my companion. I collected more images and ornaments and welcomed turtle-themed gifts from friends. Whenever I led dream workshops, I decorated a table with turtle items, along with untidy pages from my turtle notebook, as visual examples to encourage others in honoring their own dream animals.

Meanwhile, I hoped to cultivate a welcoming inner landscape where turtle might make another visit. Eleven years after *Birth Day of the Sacred Turtle* I received this gift:

Surrounded by Tortoises!

I follow a road descending a long hill to a large building. Inside, I pass an office on the left. Then I'm on an upper floor near the opening to an enclosed roof garden. Looking in, I see a scrubby, dry environment with small plants and several tortoises. The biggest tortoise, about three feet long, stands directly in front of me.

Suddenly I'm inside the roof garden, with a new perspective, looking back the way I came in. The large tortoise is now behind me and I'm facing a whole group of cute, shell-less baby tortoises. They're flesh-tone in color, chubby and friendly. At first, I'm a little worried about the reaction of the mother tortoise behind me but she doesn't seem concerned. When one baby nearby looks up at me and begins wagging its stubby little tail, I know that all is well. I'm so excited to be surrounded by all these funny, amazing babies – all this great turtle energy!

A friendly woman from the office comes into the roof garden to feed the tortoises and she tells me, "They don't begin growing their shells until age seven."

"What a great dream!" I wrote happily in the corner of this entry in my journal.

My trek down the long hill deeper into Self delivers a big payoff. Once indoors I move leftward into intuition and upward toward the divine. The roof garden reminds me of the desert mothers and fathers of the early centuries and even hints of a desert-like Garden of Eden. There I discover not only ancient turtle but an unexpected abundance of fresh energy – so new and vulnerable that it hasn't yet developed the protective housing of adulthood.

In this architectural representation of my life, an unknown part of me (a friendly wise one) comes from my control center (the office), entering the roof garden with spiritual nourishment and important information I need to know – that the turtles grow their shells at age seven. Revisiting memories from my seventh year, I reflect on increasing detachment from my mother and emergence into my unique personality. I can see how I began growing my protective shell right around that time. Additional associations for the number seven include human wholeness and deep spirituality. On a personal level, I was seven years into Twelve-Step recovery when I began exploring churches and found my way into a nourishing Christian faith.

I smiled often after this dream as I thought of my joyful encounter with those little bare-bottom baby tortoises! Then came a synchronicity almost as delightful as the dream itself.

Periodically I visit a compounding pharmacy that shares premises with a gift shop where I love to explore the dazzling displays of upscale jewelry, trinkets, décor and other wonders. One afternoon, admiring some turtle-embellished baby clothes, I spied a single copy of a *Little Golden Book* about turtles with ancient stories about how the turtle first got its shell[1]. Holding my breath lest it disappear (or someone else claim prior intention to buy it), I captured the book, ransomed it along with my husband's prescription and hurried home. In this charming compendium of ancient tales, I found my chubby, naked baby turtle. Every time I page through this storybook, I revisit one of the messages of my loveable baby tortoises: *Get back in touch with your childlike sense of joy and wonder!*

About a year and a half after *Surrounded by Tortoises*, I was diagnosed with lung cancer and embarked on several months of treatment. My friend Margie, who knew my dream recall was spotty and uninspiring, phoned one day with incredible news. She had just received a turtle dream. Knowing the Dream Maker had sent it for us both, she emailed me this incredibly vivid and detailed account:

Painted Turtles
Margie O.

I am walking back from the Patient C. Center toward the main building. I am coming from behind the building and I have to take the walkway to the left and go around to the front corner to enter. The entryway has a glass wall across the front and also along the side I just passed. When I enter, the glass wall is now on my right. There is a line of people down this side of the room and going up a staircase. There's an information desk to the left of the entrance facing the people. I show the lady at the desk the papers I got from the other building and ask her where I need to go. She says I need to get in the line and go to the fourth floor. A long line winds up the stairs.

I am standing in the line and I've moved halfway down the wall when I see a beautiful piece of art on the wall to my right. It is a painting of three sea turtles and the artist has used enamel to enhance them and lift them from the canvas. The light shining on the turtles makes them seem as if they are alive.

I realize there's activity in the center of the room. The floor is white marble and I hadn't realized before that there is a patch of white sand on the floor with a big rock in the center. As I move a little more down the line, I can see that it's not a rock at all but a huge Galapagos tortoise. A man standing next to it is unfolding a large piece of canvas. He also has buckets filled with stones of varying sizes. I look at the head of the tortoise and it turns slightly toward me and blinks its eyes. It's alive! I'd thought it was made of stone.

The man begins to sprinkle colored powders like tempera all over the back of the tortoise. Then he places the stones on top of that. I feel a little uneasy wondering what he is doing. I keep looking at the tortoise and it keeps looking at me. Then the man covers the tortoise with the canvas, leaving only his head uncovered. The man steps back and waits. As I keep moving slowly forward in the line, I wonder what he is going to do. I look back and the man steps up to the tortoise and removes the tarp. Then he begins to remove the rocks. Beautiful! The powder has turned into beautiful colors all over the back of the tortoise and they are luminous and seem almost alive. The tortoise blinks his eyes and almost seems to nod his head at me as if to say all is well.

I have just witnessed something incredibly beautiful happening with a creature that seems very patient and wise.

Dream Animal Wisdom

Stunned by this dream, I asked Margie's permission to process it as if it were my own. She agreed and we both took the dream and our processing to our next dream group meeting.

Here is my version of Margie's dream with my interpretations:

Jesus and the Tortoise

I am walking back from the part of me that is the Patient Cancer Center to the part of me that is the main building – the primary, most important manifestation of my current life. I approach from behind the building walking along the side that is a glass wall. I am pleased to see that I am becoming more open and transparent, rather than moving into one of my typical drab gray concrete dream structures. I turn a corner to the right, aware that this is all new material coming into consciousness and enter the building through another glass-walled area.

At the information desk, a woman (my inner authority) checks my papers (my identity and/or directions) and tells me to join the line with all the other people who are heading for the stairs to the fourth floor. In my dream, the fourth floor and the people in line have several layers of meaning: 1) my four rounds of chemo; 2) the countless other cancer patients who have traveled this way; 3) the great cloud of witnesses throughout Christian history as well as my own spiritual mentors and friends; 4) all the parts of myself patiently and persistently moving upward into the spiritual realm. The number four also reminds me of the four parts of human nature: intuition, feeling, thought, sensation, all of which are present in this dream. And four is the number of completion, which certainly feels true here.

When I am partway along the glass wall, moving toward the stairs, I see on my right a beautiful painting of three sea turtles swimming upward in water. The divine artist has embellished these turtles with enamel, which I've always loved, so it feels extra special to encounter my turtle in this medium. The painting is like a holy icon of the trinity with the light shining on the image seeming to bring them alive ... the three sea turtles signifying both the ocean of the unconscious as well as a "window into heaven."

Suddenly on my left intuitive side, I become aware of the divine center. This middle of the room with its white marble floor and white sand has as its center a huge Galapagos tortoise. The tortoise appears so rock-like that I think it is carved of stone but, when it blinks its eyes, I realize with surprise that it is alive! After seeing the three sea turtles on the wall, I comprehend this massive living creature as the fourth, completing the manifestation of Turtle, fully grounded in the center, a symbol of my Self.

Then I become the tortoise with Jesus beside me, unfolding his canvas for another work of art. He sprinkles colored artists' powders over my back and places stones on top of the colors. My dream ego standing in line is uneasy about this process, but my tortoise Self, the patient in need of healing, is calm. With a look, I'm able to convey that all will be well. Jesus covers my body with the canvas and steps back to wait. The spiritual transformation takes place undercover, in secret. As my dream ego continues moving forward slowly in the line by the wall, something deep and wondrous is taking place within me.

When Jesus removes the rocks and then the canvas, all can see that the colored powders have become luminous colors, almost alive in their intensity. I've received transformative healing. I blink and nod to my ego that all is well.

My dream ego can now continue on my journey after witnessing my deep healing, knowing that: 1) I have all the patience and wisdom within to complete my cancer treatments; 2) that Jesus, the Divine Healer, can transform plain, ordinary life into something of extraordinary joy, beauty and wonder; 3) that all will be well no matter how long I may live; and 4) that I've been blessed with a truly astonishing visit to my sacred center.

I devoted time to a dialog with the tortoise to see what more I might learn. I received the following: "I am Old Turtle, Wisdom, Sophia in a shell, the Ancient One. I am returning now to show you that your shell *does* serve a purpose. There are times for naked vulnerability like your shell-less baby tortoises, and there are times to celebrate in the strength and protection of the way you were created." The tortoise went on to tell me that it appeared with Jesus "for your healing and for transformation of your sight and how you view the world, your life and health and your existence in Christ. You now have transparent, glass walls and new vibrant colors." While the sea turtles in the painting on the wall indicate truths coming up from the unconscious, the giant tortoise said, "Right here, right now, I'm saying you can be transformed, made more beautiful and vibrant than ever before. But this can only happen through the process of illness and treatment – a time of being pressed down and persevering, receiving the gifts of your medical team members until your treatment process is complete."

Even the rocks that Jesus used to anchor the canvas were meaningful. As an amateur collector of rocks and minerals, I've always loved the earth's beauty. I resonated with the idea of the rocks and canvas covering the alchemical transformation of the pigments into luminous colors that harken back to the glowing little creature in *Birth Day of the Sacred Turtle*.

Margie's dream gave me much to savor as I moved from cancer patient to cancer survivor. Eventually, I began wondering if I would ever encounter Turtle myself again. Perhaps Turtle had nothing more to say directly to me.

Then came Easter morning:

Turtle on a Car

A few cars are stopped at a traffic light and I see a large turtle clinging to the back of a small, battered sedan. Afraid that it will fall off and be hurt, I hurry to knock on the driver's window. The disheveled young woman driver is dopey and impassive, so I take that for permission. I lift the turtle from the rear of the car. It's surprisingly round and at least a foot in diameter. I carry it back to the driver's window to show the woman. She just stares at it and at me. I think she must be on drugs.

I head away from the road off to the right to place the turtle near some water. The ponds there don't look particularly clean or healthy. There's a bit of sheen on the water – like oil. It seems like I'm in an industrial area, maybe near a chemical plant. I'm concerned for the turtle, but it seems like the only place where I can leave it.

What a dismal little dream for Easter! I'm dismayed by the zoned-out, asleep-at-the-wheel part of myself who is barely making it through life (stopped at a red light in a little rust-bucket car). She's oblivious to my turtle energy hanging on behind her. I remove turtle from its precarious attachment to this non-functioning part of me, only to abandon it in what seems an equally dangerous, chemically polluted environment. What sort of rescue is this?

Upon reflection, I realize that the driver, the battered car and the chemical plant highlight my post-cancer physiology – my weary body and still-recovering human chemistry. What if baptism in this pond water might leave turtle coated in an iridescent sheen – linking it to the luminous newborn turtle of my first dream and to Margie's three painted sea turtles and giant tortoise?

The mandala shape of this turtle also points toward the sacred presence that yearns to be recognized amidst the illness and suffering and pollution of the present world. The concerns and possibilities of this dream are haunting.

For a time, turtle slipped back into hiding and I missed our encounters greatly. Then as I wrote this book, I was visited once more. This time, it wasn't a pond turtle or a land tortoise who came to me, but a sea turtle, astonishingly out of his natural element:

Sea Turtle on Land

I'm looking out a window on the second floor of a building. In the area below, I see a man with a small van. Suddenly a full-grown sea turtle emerges from the back of the van and rushes toward the building where I am. I'm amazed at how fast it can move on the paved surface and I fear the rough surface will hurt its flippers.

I don't know if the man let the turtle out on purpose or by accident, but I'm worried that he will try to recapture and re-confine it, which doesn't seem right because it shouldn't be kept out of water. Then as I look out another window at right angles to the first, I see the sea turtle on the pitched roof of a neighboring building. He is angled upward, his flippers up over the edge, his back to me as he peers over the roof to see what is on the other side.

I feel deeply sad for the sea turtle desperately trying to see another possibility and being so far away from his natural home.

What might be the vista seen by my sea turtle friend? *Look outside! Look up and over and beyond what is readily seen!* How can I expand my perspective, perhaps even my worldview? It seems like a desperately courageous measure for sea turtle to venture up from my deep unconscious to navigate inhospitable ground and climb up onto one of my psychic constructs of rigid ideas and attitudes – all to show me a new way of seeing. Perhaps I can honor this encounter by shaking off presuppositions and self-imposed limitations. With courage, surely I can hoist my tentative spirit up to that rooftop, to join my sea turtle in peering over the edge to see the possibilities ahead of us.

As a dream mentor advised me years ago, I will probably see no end to the unfolding wisdom of *chelonia* in all its forms – whether tortoise, pond turtle or sea turtle. So I remain vigilant and attentive, welcoming Turtle as personal guide and archetype – my conduit to ancient wisdom that resonates but eludes definitive labeling with words.

Turtle has claimed me. I have responded. We are soul friends.

Pause

*What creature carries the energy of a personal guide for you?
How can you honor your animal companion
and bring it forth into your waking life?*

INTERLUDE
A Visitation

I expect to pass through this world but once.
Any good thing therefore that I can do,
or any kindness that I can show to any fellow creature,
let me do it now; let me not defer or neglect it,
for I shall not pass this way again.

Anonymous

Surprisingly, when I received an animal visitation dream, it was not the appearance of any one of the many cats or dogs I've counted as beloved pets. It was Graycie Green Eyes, a long-haired, gray and white feral cat of indeterminate age whom I knew and tended for only six months between our first encounter and her passing.

Here is my dream:

Graycie Green Eyes Visits Me

I'm in the center of an ambiguous space when Graycie appears. She walks toward me and I'm overjoyed that she comes directly to greet me. I'm amazed that she is alive! I'm even more surprised to see how healthy and chubby she is. After our greeting, I pet her for a few moments. Then she walks past me and away.

I first learned of Graycie's presence when a park attendant told me about her. She'd probably been around for several years, but she foraged in an area far from the main colony of community cats I tended. Assured by her ear-tip that she'd already been neutered, I said some words of thanks for that and began leaving food and fresh water for her. Being feral, she stayed at a cautious distance until I walked away. Before the cold of winter, I placed a shelter box in her area and some mornings when I arrived, I would find the towel inside still warm from her little body.

Gradually Graycie began coming closer to me and her food and I could see that she wasn't as fluffy, sturdy or nimble as she had been. By the time she let me touch her, I knew she was seriously ill. For several weeks I hopefully mixed nutritional supplements into her food and I often sat beside her on a stool to talk to her and pet her as she ate. When the day came that I lifted the frail little cat for a trip to the vet, I was heartbroken. A brief exam confirmed what I already knew. We fed her a generous last meal and released her.

I was humbled by the depth of my grief. I wept as I returned to the park to carry away her shelter box and her dishes. I wept every morning as I walked past her area. My sorrow was an aching weight I didn't fully comprehend. I'd been saddened by the death of other ferals but each of those cats had been part of a bonded group of companions. But Graycie was a loner and I was her only friend. In her decline, she had come to trust me and to accept my love and care. And through her time of need, she had been doing profound work within me.

After my dream, I returned to her in active imagination. When I told Graycie how much I had grieved, she said it was time to let her go. When I spoke of how much she had taught me about the depths of compassion, she said, *"There will be others to teach you more."*

For more than a year after Graycie's passing, I could see her trail in the grass from her feeding area to a fence where she could slip under and away to safety if she felt threatened. Her trail lingered for a long time, eventually fading as the grass rebounded in nature's healing way.

Often on my morning walks at the park, I detour briefly from my main route to visit Graycie's place. As I gaze at the spot where her shelter box and dishes stood, I re-experience the sweet energy that coursed between us, and though her grassy trail is now invisible, I treasure the indelible path of love that Graycie Green Eyes' little paws trod through my heart.

Pause

*What beloved animal has taught you about the
binding force between all creatures?
What other dream animals are now coming to teach you more?*

PART II

Focus on Themes

The most common dreams ... tend to have a "purposeful" aim (as Jung termed it) to maintain mental or even physical wellbeing. Even that aim, however, can take on many forms in attempting to achieve the more urgent needs of the dreamer and their situation – from simply restoring balance to the more ambitious aim of personality growth or individuation.

Robert Hoss

I begin each new year with a review of my previous year's dream journal. There's more to this practice than self-referential entertainment, although one's own dreams tend to be pretty fascinating stuff! I first embarked on these annual reviews to gain an overview of what my psyche had been up to all year and to update my index of dream animals and other symbols. Soon I discovered myself snaring the golden threads of recurring themes that I'd missed as the dreams occurred. Typically this annual practice kindles a new burst of excitement for the upcoming year's dreaming and reminds me to watch for these threads with insistent vibration.

In Part II we turn our attention toward underlying ideas and motifs. The dreams clustered in upcoming chapters showcase a variety of creatures, all busy in service to their dreamers. These chapters have taken shape around thematic nuclei evident in my dreams, in dreams of my group members and in dreams submitted for this book. Fortuitously the content and significance of several contributed dreams generated the creation of two chapters not in my initial plan.

So how do our dream animals convey the themes our psyches want to illuminate for us? An example may prove helpful.

A theme that recurs throughout my dream journals I call *Lost and Injured in the City*. As illustrated in the previous *Cats* chapter, I'm well conversant with the appearances of hurt or neglected dream animals as snapshots about my current level of self-care. Here that motif is expanded and sharpened with wild animals wandering through inhospitable urban settings. Three brief samples: *I dream of an injured baby dinosaur (a cute little plant-eater with a neck frill and nose horn) running between cars to reunite with its mother and siblings, who all then make their way safely together across a busy intersection. I dream of a black panther running loose in a city, with one rear leg dangling, a useless bare bone ending in a knob where the big cat's foot should be. I dream of a lost baby bear with scruffy brown fur sticking out in clumps, sniffing about the city streets, desperately looking for something to eat.*

The theme linking my *Lost and Injured in the City* dreams: the collective (the city) is simply not where I best thrive. My deep instincts suffer, longing for a place of security, rest and nourishment when I have been spending too much of my waking life in extraversion. I see this is an old pattern (the dinosaurs). Even meaningful pursuits can unground me (the big cat's useless leg and missing foot) and leave me neglected and starving (the poor baby bear) at a deep psychic level *if* they keep me too long outside myself in the community and the larger world.

An extrovert reader may find this a bizarre or even laughable interpretation; the introvert may better understand. That is as it should be. Even with the help and support of dream groups and mentors, we must all finally name the truths of our own dreams.

Hopefully, this brief example and the chapters that follow will help you notice and identify the motifs that already reside among the creatures in your dream world.

Spiritual Menagerie

All things bright and beautiful,
all creatures great and small,
all things wise and wonderful:
the Lord God made them all.

Cecil Frances Alexander

Somewhere along my meandering spiritual journey, my love for art and my late-blooming faith coalesced into appreciation for the earliest form of Christian art, sacred icons, and quietly, insistently these quaintly stylized images infiltrated my morning devotional times. Leafing through an icon catalog one day, I spotted depictions of Jesus creating the animals – the prologue to the gospel of John rendered in imagery. "Through him all things were made; without him nothing was made that has been made." (John 1:3) My favorite of these icons depicts Jesus, the Christ, extending his hand over a throng of creatures, including some rib-tickling renditions of exotic animals the artist obviously had never seen. These ageless images continue prompting me to reflect on the place of humans and all the creatures within the web of creation.

At my first major dream conference, the keynote speaker mentioned how common it is for new dreamworkers to be abundantly blessed by spiritual dreams, where one needn't coax out a spiritual meaning, but the spiritual message is the dream's central element. Her words affirmed my own experience and helped to reinforce the synergy between my growing dreamwork practice and my faith.

This chapter features overtly spiritual dreams. We begin with an unnerving nightmare recorded in my first dream journal, which gives new meaning to the old phrase "people who live in glass houses":

Constance Bovier

The Grizzly Bear

I am with other people in the woods and we are all conscious of a great danger from a grizzly bear. We are living in this bear's territory. The others go to their home further uphill. I arrive at my house, a long rectangle surrounded by windows and glass doors. My mother is sitting in a chair talking on the phone when the grizzly bear appears at a window. I am terrified as the bear moves from window to window, glaring in at us. Mother never gets out of her chair or shows any distress. She is talking calmly to another family and finally mentions that the bear is here at our house.

I am frantic! I know my father is upstairs and he could help me. But I can't find any stairs to climb. Finally, I swing along a row of jungle gym-like bars on the ceiling till I reach an entry to the second floor. Father is napping there. I wake him and he gets up to come and help. I feel reassured and relieved.

As a new dreamworker, I was still anxious when raw emotions erupted so powerfully. In this dream, my frenzied dream ego is frustrated at the calmer part of me (my mother) who seems guided by something I don't know how to access as she communicates with another part of me. Nor do I know how to reach the father figure (God), a literal reference to "the man upstairs." It isn't easy at this point for me to reach God (as my spiritual director and I discussed). No clear path (traditional stairway) exists, so I have to be creative and persistent to get there.

Of course, all this begs the question: What am I running from with such terror? After all, I'm living in bear territory and in a glass house. What might one expect? All of the windows are offering me a new perspective, but I'm not ready to deal with that. In this case, unable to engage this powerful, wild energy (I can't even meet the bear's fierce gaze through a window) and unwilling to adopt the placid (or oblivious) modeling of my mother, I flee toward a spiritual solution. This dream occurred long before I understood that welcoming and engaging my dream animals was *not* something to be avoided, but an essential part of my spiritual growth.

My journal notes indicate that at that period in my life I had much enthusiasm for what I was encountering in waking life, but this dream shows clearly that something was chasing me at a deep level and that seeking help *from upstairs* was my answer.

♥

In contrast, I invite you into a peaceful dream experience, also featuring windows. This dreamer was midway through her spiritual director training program and relatively new to dreamwork when this dream arrived. With its memorable tableau and robust energy, it provided ample encouragement for her ongoing commitment to dreams:

Encounter with Inner Wolf
Anne Carlton Johnson

I am walking in a beautiful green manicured yard, with boxwood hedges and lovely trees to my left. It's dusk, just as the sun is going down. Above the trees in the distance, I see beautiful mountains with spectacular colors – gold, purple, bronze and orange. A big dog is walking at my right side, but I know it's not my dog. We are walking toward a friend's house to check on it because my friend is on vacation. The house is a stately traditional brick home.

All of a sudden, the dog crouches down, staring at something in the distance. I look where the dog is looking and I see a figure approaching, weaving in and out of the brush at the base of the mountains. As it gets closer, I realize it's a wolf. It keeps coming closer and somehow evades the dog, circles around us and stops in front of us. Suddenly it is standing right in front of me, looking me directly in my face. I'm not afraid but I just stare into the eyes of the wolf.

Then I continue into the house, the dog with me. There are a beautiful cathedral ceiling and a huge picture window where I can continue looking at the colorful mountains. I start moving three chairs from the back of the large room to the window where I can sit and enjoy the beauty in front of me. While I am doing this, I feel undertones and sense movement going on around me. I'm not fearful, but I know it is there.

Anne found the verdant setting for her dream particularly inviting. She feels that her dog companion might belong to her friend who was away, and the absence of this personality fragment places Anne's ego into the central role in the scene. The large dog is unfamiliar to her (her waking life dogs are Corgis), representing new energy coming into consciousness (from the right side).

Anne's intense concentration on shadow work at the time of this dream strongly informs her interpretation. "I think the wolf is my shadow that has been at the base of the mountain and is now slowly moving (weaving in and out of view) into my conscious. The unfamiliar dog may be what has been protecting me up to now from really looking at my shadow side. It also says that I haven't yet tapped into a larger life."

Anne's close-up encounter with her wolf holds incredible spiritual power. The time is right for this engagement which happens without fear on Anne's part or aggression between the two creatures. In an embracing movement, the wolf draws a mandala around Anne and the dog, highlighting this moment as an engagement with the Self. Then the wolf and Anne simply gaze at one another.

"The eye contact was a soul thing," she said. "It was amazing, beautiful and spiritual – so humbling that this animal could somehow be in contact with me."

After that moment passes and the wolf disappears, Anne and the dog enter the house (her life/psyche), represented as a lovely, Williamsburg-like home, emphasizing Anne's love for genealogy and warm appreciation for ancestors and history. The spiritual realm she enters (the cathedral ceiling and the trinity of ordinary chairs) offer commentary on her religious/spiritual life and its relevance to her. Sitting on one of the three chairs before the huge picture window, she is likely to gain an entirely new perspective. "In the view of the green plants, the woods and the beautiful mountains, I see what awaits me when I can acknowledge those parts of my psyche that need my attention," she said.

At the end of this dream, Anne feels strength in the sensed movement around her. "Even with the undertones, I am at ease. I realize that at my age my journey here on this earth is fast approaching an end but seeing that the future is so beautiful and peaceful, I can sit on that chair and enjoy the view of what awaits me."

Amy Curran, whose spider dream appears in the *Bugs* chapter, shares here her relationship with another creature. "Turtle launched me into the unconscious," she said. After reading a newspaper article about dreams, Amy sought out the writer and joined her newly forming dream group where each person drew a card from a deck of power animals. "That animal would become a guide in helping us to access our dreams and make meaning of the inner journey we were embarking on."

When Amy drew the sea turtle card, she felt the ancient creature had chosen her. "The turtle was being called into my waking conscious life to prepare me for a profound change in my personal growth and spiritual awakening." The sea turtles' ability to emerge from the womb of a sandy shore and to swim in the depths of the ocean became a metaphor for Amy's deep dive into the unconscious in preparation for rebirth.

A rich period of synchronicities followed as she found signs and symbols all around her. At a costume event, Amy dressed as the mythological St. George who journeyed to find and slay a dragon. "As fate would have it, this fairy tale had connections to the characteristics of my newly established power animal," she said, noting that both George and the sea turtle traveled over land and sea and both have shields for protection.

All of her group members hoped to receive a dream from their power animals and Amy was delighted when she did:

The Acquaintance
Amy Curran

I am swimming down a river with snow-covered mountains to my right that drop down into the river. It is nighttime. The water is flowing fast and I'm being propelled around large, smooth rocks, some sticking up out of the rapids. I feel like the river is beginning to take me too fast and pull me under. But I'm able to stop myself and the next thing I know, I'm swimming underwater heading upstream.

I look over my left shoulder and see sea turtles swimming along with me! I reach out and touch the back of one and am amazed at how his shell is solid but soft and rubbery as well. I am approached by three different turtles. The first two I don't recognize, but when the third approaches me, I reach out and touch his smooth neck and peer into his face. He is friendly and I feel a connection as though I know him. When I ask him if he is the one, he nods his head and looks back at me. My eyes follow his and I'm sure there is a connection to something he knows.

"I knew this turtle had to be an aspect of me – so wise and knowing," Amy said. "I was intent on understanding with my eyes, being able to see underwater what he knew." That same week when she found a hand-carved sandstone sea turtle that reminded her of her dream, she bought the little turtle and named him George. "Now George sits above my desk where I can often gaze into his knowing eyes."

Shortly after this dream, on a trip to Mexico, Amy participated at a sea turtle sanctuary as newly hatched turtles began their instinctive trek toward the ocean. "I felt fortunate to participate in the process of launching these small yet determined sea creatures. Looking back, my power animal seemed to be preparing me for the process of launching my own four children who had all recently left the nest at home, as well as the process of discovering my deep inner self. The turtle gave me insight into the importance of diving down into the depths of my unconscious and it reminds me of the promise of rebirth."

This powerful experience in Amy's early dreamwork journey continues to guide and inform her.

Water has been a powerful metaphor in my dream world as well, typically arriving as a compelling invitation, always reminding me that the unconscious is a place of divine encounter.

In this relatively recent dream I had no choice but to dive in:

Divine Encounter

I'm standing on a dock with an unseen companion. The water is full of alligators, submerged but visible. They are short and wide with broad legs. I don't see their heads and I think how much they resemble logs. But clearly, the water is dangerous. Then the water begins rising and I start to retreat but something in me says, "No! It's time to go in!"

I move into the water and instantly my awareness is filled by a large image, like an MRI of my own brain activity, brilliant and sparkling. I know that I am with God. I feel joy-filled, "right," amazed, happy and grateful. I sense distractions trying to pull me away, but I am able to ignore them, and I remain in the sense of union with the divine for fully two or three minutes before I awaken, astounded.

This profound and numinous encounter centers on the fearsome, primitive alligator – an ancient presence that resides within my depths whether or not I wish it to be there. I've jokingly referred to my reptilian brain and, lo and behold, here it is on mega wattage! Yet only after I'm willing to step into the unknown dangers of the alligator-infested water (my fears) can I be present to the mystical experience that awaits.

To me it is telling that the image shows my brain (not my heart, as I might prefer), alluding perhaps to my dependence upon the intellect. Even so, it reminds me that the divine can engage me at any level, and my psyche can embody God-consciousness with whatever imagery it chooses. So I treasure this alligator dream as a direct revelation of holy mystery.

Sometimes the Dream Maker behaves like an entertainment producer who knows the value of ensembles. Just like a movie may gather up a select group of admired actors, our animal dreams may enlist a variety of creatures to tell a story.

The following dream began for me in a spacious sanctuary where elaborate preparations were underway for a big church event. After leaving that area, I suddenly find myself in an adjacent building:

Where is my Energy?

I am upstairs in a huge, attic-like space that's divided into big rooms. Many children are present and then I see the animals. At first, I see birds everywhere, walking about, many sizes and varieties, mostly black and white. Then I'm in another room farthest away from the entry where I see many small mammals. A teacher talks with me and says there's usually a cat there. I look into a box with a cushion, but there's no cat.

Back near the door, I encounter two large cats. I talk to one – a long-haired cat with mixed pastel colors. I reach out to pet it and it grabs my hand with its claws extended. I pull away, disappointed and find a tiny restroom where I'm able to wash and disinfect the scratches on my hands. Then a friend from church tells me that eleven cats live in this place but they're all sad and unsettled right now because the dog has died.

Because this dream spontaneously provided its own title, I surmise that those words pose the central question. Beginning in a deep part of myself (a sunken, theater-style sanctuary), I then move upward to a high place, a pilgrimage of sorts, where I find animals living together in a unique version of a peaceable kingdom. So it seems at first.

I'm aware that there's much for me to learn here (a teacher is present). First, the birds (spiritual in nature) are black and white. While this suggests that I may have some rigid (black and white) thinking about religion, it feels truest to me that they point toward a union of opposites and an integration of conscious and unconscious material.

Naturally, I gravitate toward the cat energy that's so familiar to me. But all is not well. The first cat is missing from its box. My attempt to befriend another cat results in an injury that I must look after to avoid infection. Significantly I learn that eleven cats live there. Eleven is known as a master number with a connection to the unconscious, to gut feelings and knowledge without rational thought. This rings true for me because here I face an aggressive aspect of cat that I've not come upon in other dreams.

This dream offers a valuable visit to my internal warehouse of energies which feels inextricably linked to the divine. Here I learn that it's time to look beyond feline energy to other instincts with which I may not yet be as familiar. I see a cautionary ending in that the part of me represented by a dog has died, warning me that without that loyal, relational canine energy, I can be far out of balance. Other truths await.

To close our spiritual menagerie chapter, I offer a final brief ensemble dream:

Pebbles and the Bird

In the entryway by my front door, I discover why my housecats have been acting so strangely. A large complex spider web hangs high on the wall near the ceiling. In the web is a dove. Suddenly what had appeared to be a spider's web becomes a bird's nest. Astonishingly my little female cat Pebbles is up there beside the nest and she is lovingly nuzzling the bird.

This dream was a delight as well as a surprise! Synchronously a pigeon and her newly hatched babies were nesting above our kitchen window on the slender casing of a rolling storm shutter. Yet their nest was hardly as precarious a perch as this dream's impossible nesting spot high on a bare wall in our front entry. How could a nest, bird and cat all be suspended there? Well, dreams, as has been said of drama, require a suspension of disbelief.

Pebbles with her sweet disposition – a great contrast to our bolder male cats – seems a suitable representation of the divine feminine. Here she rises up into communion with Spirit, embodied in the dove. While the appearance of a *complex* spider web indicates one of my complexes is at work, it also suggests the cosmic weaving of my life.

I see in this dream a tender and memorable snapshot of my individuation at that moment – an integration of my deep instinctual self, the divine feminine (cat), the Spirit (dove) and home (nest), all cast against the archetypal web of life. Who could ask for more?

Pause

*How have you experienced the numinous in your dreams?
In what ways have your dream creatures
participated in your divine encounters?*

Diamonds in the Details

*As did Jung, I find four-ness to be one of the most
important imagery patterns in dreams.
The four motif appears frequently in dreams as
square or rectangular shapes and objects,
such as the shape of a room, a building, or a table.
Jung related the motif of four or four-ness
to the process of individuation, a state of completion,
a pattern or order and stability,
often representing a solution or closure.*

Robert Hoss

Spellbound, I circled the conference room at the Jung Center of Houston, marveling at the framed paintings on the walls – a fiery bear, a catlike old woman, a pair of winged fish-humans, big cats, snakes and a host of imaginary creatures. I couldn't wait to see and learn more. I went home that day with a book from the Jung Center library and spent hours savoring the remarkable paintings of Peter Birkhäuser[1]. A commercially successful fine artist, Birkhäuser segued into depicting his dream images during his many years in analysis with the earliest Jungians in Switzerland. Today I have my own copy of his book and I remain enthralled by paintings like his *Imprisoned Power,* in which an enormous black beast stands encased in a fiery, crumbling mountain ... or over-wrought smoldering brain. In the foreground we see a minuscule man abandoning his tiny car at the base of this ominous apparition, fleeing in terror.

Birkhäuser's evocative paintings have helped me formulate clarifying questions to ask myself during and after journaling a dream, among them being: *What does my dream creature really look like?* Priceless value lies in the details of size, number, color, shape, sound and other specifics. In this chapter, we'll see how carefully recorded details often spark a dreamer's understanding and, in some cases, even embody a dream's meaning.

While it's always best to plumb personal associations first, I recommend two fine resources to help trigger further awareness about details: Robert Hoss's *Color Questionnaire*[2] and Doris Snyder's *Numbers in Dreams*[3].

The following brief dream from my journals illustrates the value of size, color and number in a single image:

Three Big Black Animals

I am facing three huge black animals. To the left is a bull. In the center is a dog, a black Labrador. On the right is a horse. The dog approaches me, and I am very cautious.

These three larger-than-life creatures represent unknown material (black) coming from the unconscious and suggest for me the trinity as well as mythological meanings. The flanking creatures feel Biblical in their strength and power, with the dog the sole connection to my own life and world. Yet this traditionally friendly black Lab intimidates me with its movement and I'm wary and anxious in the presence of these massive archetypical creatures.

Besides this trio, my journals contain other overly large creatures: *I'm looking over a ridiculously flimsy, low fence into a wildlife park as three enormous bears rush forward.* Another example: *I see an enormous bird so weighted down with colorful decorations that it can't fly. To my chagrin, I know this bird represents self-aggrandizement.* Awakening, I recalled what our wonderful dream teacher Jeremy Taylor so often said – that our dreams *don't* come to support our egos.

Of course, not all of our resized animals are enormous archetypes, magnified energies or ego inflations. Some dream creatures are miniature versions of their real selves as we see in the following two dreams shared by Kate B., a retired therapist and dedicated dreamworker:

Filthy Woolly Mammoths
Kate B.

An old friend comes to visit me. My house has an impersonal, motel-like feel as if It's not mine. The woman from the large house across the way comes toward us. Some troublesome things have been going on over there and she tells us about frightening phone calls. She is scared. As we look toward her place, all of a sudden, we see three filthy, shaggy woolly mammoths emerge from the ground beneath her yard and start running around. They are the size of small ponies, but they look mean. We run back to my house and we are safe.

Initially resistant to working with this dream, Kate finally engaged it, first by imagining a new ending. She discovered that she felt compassion for the little mammoths and how they had lived, and wanted to help them. In active imagination, she asked the woman who lived across the street if they could trade houses. The woman agreed, so Kate left the house that didn't feel like hers anyway and went to live in the other one. Then she arranged for someone to come help her clean up the little mammoths. She built a large fenced area where she could tend to them and get to know them.

To give her dream voice, Kate used the Magic Questions. Here's what she learned by embodying a small woolly mammoth:

1. I am one of three woolly mammoths. I'm glad to be moving around after being part of the landscape for so long.
2. My purpose is to let Kate know that I'm alive and that if she just lets me roam around, I can be helpful. I'm super-strong, big and dependable and I've been around for ages. She can use my help.

3. I like that I'm an ancient source of strength.
4. I don't like that I may look foreboding or brutish so I got "frozen out" and made part of the landscape. But I'm alive and part of this whole.
5. What I fear most is that I'll be frozen out and made into the landscape again. That's when I get dirty and look scary and foreboding.
6. What I desire most is that Kate looks at her tendency to cast me aside and open up to more messages about why and how she froze me out.
7. My message to Kate is: *Open up and listen in your heart to your source of strength.*

As Kate worked with her dream, she began to recognize some old, historical patterns of thinking and being that she'd kept buried. She feels that the underlying message is her propensity to believe that she's done wrong, *been* wrong, and been inadequate, all of which has furthered her resistance to entertaining the possibility that she has an authentic source of deep strength.

Notice that Kate's powerful energy bursts forth in triad form in a yard that she doesn't even recognize as her own ... until her subsequent active imagination. The woman in the larger house (a fragment of Kate) is already disturbed by communications from Kate's unconscious (troublesome things and frightening phone calls). We can imagine the roiling unsettledness as Kate's buried energy prepares to cut loose, erupting mightily in the front yard. Imagine three pony-size mammoths rushing about, probably trumpeting their joy at release, stomping and shaking the dirt from their faces, after bursting into the light!

Kate recognizes the mammoth trinity's important commentary on her wellbeing. "I don't tend to my spiritual life well enough, so it slips back into the landscape, still alive, but not active and nourished. My spiritual connection often isn't strong or consistent enough for me to be open to this source of vibrant energy."

Through engagement with this dream, Kate continued relating to her washed, brushed and well-nourished little mammoths, open to what they came to offer her.

A year later, she had another dream featuring smaller-than-actual creatures:

Miniature Turkey Buzzards
Kate B.

While walking, I see a few miniature turkey buzzards that are the size of small birds. A man tells me that there are too many of them, a possible infestation. I begin to notice more of them. Some are even floating on the water like ducks. Back at home, a man who looks like my father is typing out information about the buzzards. I say that's good and that he should research the legal and governmental aspects of what we can do. A neighbor is taking pictures and I am going to figure out how to reach other people who may need help.

In this dream, Kate retreats from an actual encounter with the unwelcome vulture energy and intellectualizes it instead, seeking external solutions to the *infestation*. As with insects in dreams, this multitude might be considered a single creature – a dark, unfamiliar intrusion for which Kate seeks a heady, official (legal, governmental) solution. She appears to have plenty of help, with various parts of her personality pitching in.

Since these mini birds reminded Kate of her little mammoths, she also explored the possibility of her diminutive creatures as a reflection of her waking life energy, which is often severely restricted by an autoimmune disease.

My dream journals also have revealed some unusually small creatures. On one occasion, I enter my dream house to be confronted by a family of bad-tempered miniature hippos. What wild energy was galumphing around within me that night?

The following dream offered me some penetrating insights from a small tiger and a thin stuffed animal:

Tiger in the Road

My husband and I are driving along a road when we see a small tiger (about the size of a large dog) lying in the road. We stop because I can see it breathing. As we get out of the car, I see two tiger cubs lying nearby. We walk toward a house on the right and the adult tiger gets up and follows us, apparently unhurt. In the house, I am confused about which of several stuffed animals there belonged to me and which belong to the other residents. I finally choose a skinny version of Minnie Mouse, deciding that it must be the one that was mine.

A dog-sized tiger seems relatively benign, however, this one is lying right in the path of my progress causing me to stop and pay attention. New possibilities lie nearby (the two cubs). Fortunately, the miniature tiger is unhurt, but it seems to have a mission and follows me to the house where I go indoors, back to my introvert's comfort zone.

The living tiger energy remains outside while I move deeper into my psyche/life where I find myself surrounded by artificial energies (the stuffed animals). I'm uncertain about who (what part of me) owns these static, unrealized instincts. Nor am I sure which one has been mine at an earlier time. At the end of the dream, I choose an anorexically thin Minnie Mouse.

When asked by my dream group why I chose that particular stuffed creature, my spontaneous reply surprised them and deeply shocked me: "Because that's all I'm entitled to."

Who are the other aspects of myself that I'm willing to put ahead of my own needs or desires? How long have I been living small – in an unsubstantial, enfeebled mouse-like way – when I need only step outside of myself to claim a living, vibrant tiger energy? How might I encourage growth in the tiger mother and embrace the possibilities inherent in her two cubs, waiting at the side of the road where I can resume my life journey?

Like Kate with her small mammoths and buzzards, I've discovered that my dream animals can mirror fluctuations in my psychic and physiological energy. In 2017 at the beginning of my journey through lung cancer, my daughter gave me a delightful *Animalia* coloring journal, bursting with the wildly creative art of Kerby Rosannes.[4] This journal and my colored pencils accompanied me to all of my medical appointments where the realistic and fantastical little creatures added much humor to the long periods in waiting rooms. Before my initial biopsy results, I wrote: *"Last night I dreamed of a lion the same size as the lion on this page!"*

Tiny Lion

I have a very small male lion. It's adult in form, but the size of a domestic kitten. It's so wild that I can't control it or make it stop biting and scratching when handled. I am preparing to take the little lion to be euthanized because no one can manage it. But I wonder if I might find a lion sanctuary where it could grow up.

Part of me knows this ferocious little fellow has the potential for enlargement, but I'm having enough trouble it seems with its current size. This dream brings forward my familiar struggle with a controlling nature and my ongoing efforts to subdue, ignore or eliminate wild instincts. There's little surprise in this as I was dealing with a new level of powerlessness in confronting cancer. In subsequent months other dream creatures joined forces with the entertaining animals in my journal, accompanying me through radiation and chemotherapy. On one two-page spread, I labeled each of the gamboling monkeys with the various side effects of my chemo.

After treatment, when life settled down to periodic scans, I had a long dream about cleaning and remodeling my house – a predictable commentary on my physical wellbeing – which then shifted to this scene:

Abandoned Industrial Plant

I'm driving to an isolated place when I see a male lion high up on a cliff to the right. He appears quite small because of the distance. A voice tells me that there are cougars and leopards there too. Stopping my car, I enter a building that seems like an abandoned industrial plant. As I walk through the first level to head upstairs, I pass a gaping square hole in the middle of the floor. I'm concerned that a dog might run about and fall in.

During my illness and recovery, I'd relinquished a number of my former activities (abandoned industry). Returning now to this space, I see a powerful lion and learn of other big cat energies far in the distance, all limited in size but suggesting available energies on the horizon. Inside my life where lots of things used to get done, I encounter a noteworthy central image, the square symbol of wholeness – a literal hole – in the middle of the floor.

What might I find if I were to seek a way down into that space, into the core of myself which has been deserted for a time? And what if I were to call upon the loyal companionship of an off-stage dog to accompany me?

❣

We move now from looking at animal sizes to considering dream creatures in vividly colorful garb.

When Margie O. had been involved in SoulCollage^R for about a year, she joined a weekly group to share and discuss their SoulCollage cards and, consequently, became more intentional about her practice.[5] "I tend to be a thinker, more logical," she said, "but I had just spent an entire day making cards, creating constantly for hours, and I'd been deep into my feelings." This is the context into which Margie's psyche presented this dream:

Helping at the Pet Store
Margie O.

I'm in a one-room pet store, a deep rectangular building the size of a mobile home with a door at one end. There are two snakes and a parrot among other creatures. One snake is slender and about two feet long. The other is about five feet long with a thick body and a two-toned brown pattern. I have a long rod with a crooked end like a shepherd's hook for moving the snakes. I don't work here but I'm temporarily in charge while the owner is out.

A man comes in and he wants to go to the fish tank at the back of the store. There's only one aisle leading from the door to the back of the store. I have to caution him not to step on the big snake that is stretched out in a straight line in the aisle. I use the rod to move the snake to the side. I don't see the smaller snake. The man goes back to the fish and then leaves after a bit. Then the beautiful scarlet macaw squawks. I hold out my hand and call to him to see what he will do.

After a few minutes, he flies over, lands on my arm and looks at me. He is very heavy, but I don't want him to leave.

♥

"There is only one path in the pet store," she said. "The aisle goes straight from the door all the way back to the fish tanks (the water of the unconscious/the water of baptism). For Margie, the rectangular shape of the store highlights an imbalance in thinking versus feeling as opposed to the greater stability of a square. "Yet here the shape has a positive focus, directing me toward the spiritual and emotional rather than the logical – overthinking everything."

When the unknown man enters, he is intent on walking directly to the deepest point of the store. Interestingly the large snake is not coiled but extends along the aisle (a masculine presentation of the serpent) as if pointing the way. Margie, being there to tend all the diverse instinctual energies in the shop, cautions the man and uses her shepherd's hook (a reference to Jesus, the good shepherd) to move the snake so it won't be stepped on by the masculine.

In her research, Margie discovered that snakes commonly emerge when a dreamer has been involved in significant creativity, as she'd been with SoulCollage. She added that her dream snakes represent duality. "To me, the large snake is the spiritual, and its brown color points toward my true self and my natural state of being. The shorter snake, which appears at the beginning, represents the emotions." Significantly her usually dominant logic is absent; it's not needed (or wanted) in this rich storehouse of instinctual energies.

The dream ends with the marvelously showy scarlet macaw, a hefty bird that boldly wears the four primary colors. Margie learned that Carl Jung associated red with feeling, yellow with intuition, blue with thinking and green with sensation. A balanced pattern of these four colors in a dream can indicate an evolving state of completion within the personality.

In waking life, Margie has felt the living weight of a macaw on her arm when meeting a friend's bird and on a mission trip to the

Amazon. Here she receives the weight of her dream bird's message through their eye contact. "I had been in my feelings all of the previous day," she said. "But the macaw with its four primary colors is bringing me the message of balance. And I want to hold onto that!"

This wonderfully affirming dream gave Margie a look at some powerful wisdom at her disposal. We might imagine the Dream Maker as the off-stage owner of the pet store. And we might assume that Margie will be welcome to help out there at any time. In fact, with the shop's similarity to a mobile home, she can probably take this portable warehouse of spiritual and emotional energies along with her wherever she goes.

Our final dream highlighting color comes from Steve Wilkerson[6], a retired physician and long-time dreamworker with an advanced degree in mythology. Steve is among the contemporary Jungians inspired by Carl Jung's alchemical studies to delve into this realm for themselves. His deep knowledge of mythology and alchemy coalesced in this vividly archetypal, yet uniquely personal, dream:

Engaging Cerberus
Steve Wilkerson

I return from work and enter my home, where I see a large dog with three heads in front of the living room couch. The dog is entirely a bright, nearly iridescent red. It begins barking at me as soon as I enter. I'm afraid I may be attacked, so I kick the dog away.

As soon as I make contact with the dog, it turns into a smiling baby that I'm holding in my arms. The baby is wrapped in a white blanket covered with light blue and green figures. It appears to be just a few months old, about two feet long, possibly longer, yet it is very light, almost weightless. The baby looks at my face and begins laughing. It then immediately turns into a black raven, caws, and flies away.

♥

Steve quickly recognized the dog as Cerberus, the fearsome three-headed dog of Greek mythology. "Cerberus guards the gates of the underworld, Hades, to prevent the dead from leaving there." Here Cerberus greets Steve right in the center of his own home (his psyche), rising to its feet in front of the living room couch (a place of rest). All three heads bark fiercely and three pairs of eyes glare at him. The dog's task in the dream is to guard what is hidden. "For me, the underworld is my unconscious and I have some resistance about coming in contact with the unconscious material because it's new."

Steve cites the myth that features Cerberus along with the famous mythological Greek hero, Heracles (Hercules). The last of the twelve labors of Heracles was to capture Cerberus and bring him up from the underworld to earth. While Heracles doesn't appear in the dream, the implications of his off-screen presence are significant. Steve equates Heracles with the Self, suggesting that he will have all the strength and power necessary to meet and manage any material that Cerberus is attempting to keep down in his unconscious.

Steve's apprehension about learning something new about himself is conveyed by his kicking the dog aside – something he would never do to a real dog in waking life. While this seems a necessary protective action, this instant of physical contact triggers the first transformation.

Suddenly Cerberus disappears and Steve holds a sizeable baby that is clearly Spirit (without substance or weight). He spends the majority of his time in this high-energy dream cuddling the baby. "It's a powerful time of transition and it is wonderful. I absolutely love the baby's laughter!" Relating this experience to his waking life enjoyment of his infant granddaughter, he said the eye contact with the dream baby is spiritually profound, "like looking at the eyes of the soul and seeing God."

The next change occurs abruptly. "When the weightless baby transforms, it becomes a raven that flies away." Steve noted that all movement within the dream is upward from the dog on the floor to the baby in his arms to the raven in the air – from earthly grounding to things of the spirit. "It's definitely an alchemical progression."

This dream fairly pulsates with energy and symbolism. First, looking at colors from his passionate interest in alchemy, Steve said, "Alchemists were never interested in turning lead into gold. They were interested in healing for the sick, the possibility of eternal life, and many were interested in spiritual transformation. The gold the alchemists were searching for is emblematic of a new life." So an alchemical transformation is, in essence, a spiritual one. "Classically, the transformation process goes from black to white to red," he explained. "But you can begin anywhere because the process is a spiral. You keep going through this pattern over and over. Ideally, it brings the ego closer to Self."

Because Steve's dream begins with the red Cerberus, "It emphasizes its deep alchemical nature by stepping out of the ordinary sequence." Red, the Latin *rubedo* of alchemy, is a personally powerful metaphor. As a retired physician, Steve immediately associates red with blood and life energy. The bright red dog seems to glow, and the word *iridescent* in the dream narrative isn't merely happenstance. "That word comes from the Greek goddess Iris, the goddess of the rainbow (multiple colors), another mythological association representing life energy. Also, Iris is closely related to Hermes in that they are messengers from the Gods to human beings. That is what is happening here – the God within me is communicating through color and Iris/iridescence."

The baby with its white (Latin *albedo*) blanket constitutes the second alchemical color. "Of course, it's also the white of Christianity," said Steve. "Though your sins may be scarlet or black, when you're pardoned, your soul shall be as white as snow." The figures on the baby's blanket introduce new colors and elements. Steve's far-ranging associations with blue include school colors as well as ocean and sky. "Green for me definitely is new life." He described the figures on the blanket as "positive, fun-loving, mischievous little elves with kindly faces. The elf is a classic trickster figure. But you can trick someone in two ways. You can take advantage and make them miserable or you can trick them into finding out new information about themselves." Here again, Steve senses the presence of the mythological Hermes: "When Hermes tricks people, it's for their own benefit." Trickster energy in this dream provides an exquisitely human interlude of joy and laughter before the final transformation when baby becomes raven who flies away.

Raven, the largest of the blackbird family, carries powerful associations. Black (Latin *nigredo*) is a complicated color with contrasting meanings and energies. Steve relates to the Biblical story in which the recalcitrant Jonah undergoes a time of darkness in the "great fish" (see Jonah 1-2), with black representing the night before the change. Symbolically the raven often represents dark angels, elemental spirits and certainly death and putrefaction. Steve pointed to Edgar Allan Poe's unforgettable poem, *The Raven*, with its haunting refrain, *"Quoth the Raven 'Nevermore'."* His fleeting moments with the raven are profound: "Here the raven is the messenger of death, but I am dying in order to be reborn."

Steve's dream also showcases the importance of numbers and Jung's emphasis on quaternity. "The number three is masculine, the number of activity. The number four is feminine, the number of completion." One also might look at fairy tales and many modern examples such as three-act plays in which a story is told in threes, with the denouement providing the fourth, concluding element.

"In my dream, the number three points toward the future," Steve said. Three figures (dog, baby, raven), three heads on the dog, three colors on the baby's blanket. The raven itself is one of three birds in the earliest story of the flood, the Epic of Gilgamesh, in which a dove, swallow and raven are sent out. And it's a common figure in the progression through the alchemical colors where birds such as raven, swan and phoenix are sometimes used. With four, the completion, the unconscious is no longer threatened with being overwhelmed."

Steve sees the gift of this dramatic dream as a re-creation, the beginning of a new chapter in life. "In the dream, I'm coming home from a boring office job, metaphorical for my need to transition from where I am in life now. I'm entering a new era of life with a birthday coming so I'm facing an enormous transition, physically, psychologically and spiritually, and I have to make a change in my attitude about that." For example, as a long-time teacher of adults, Steve recently began tutoring grade school children – a rewarding venture in a completely new direction.

"The dream is asking what I will do now," he said, "now that I know all this? I'm exploring new possibilities and asking where I should spend my time and place my energy. I'm not going to stay dead. It's time for an important transformation."

Pause

What feelings stir within you as you write a detailed description of your dream animal? Which of these details are essential in conveying your creature's messages?

Who's in Charge Here?

*The mix of masculine and feminine might condense
in a dream scene to represent a conflict
relating to an imbalance or over-identification
with one or the other inner attributes.
A balanced whole personality might be considered to
consist of an equal mix of the two characteristics,
whereby either can be accessed readily when
needed to deal with a life situation.*

Robert Hoss

Some marvelously rich dreamwork takes place in the gender landscape. As women begin learning about their inner masculine energy (the *animus* in Jungian parlance) and men about their inner feminine (the Jungian *anima*), we may discover all sorts of balance/imbalance, dominance/passivity and other issues. In speaking of masculine-feminine tensions, I'm referring to the frequent disparities between the more logical, structured, goal-oriented, problem-solving part of the psyche and the more nurturing, feeling-oriented, relational, intuitive part. Regardless of one's gender orientation, we have all these capacities within us, and they often express themselves in dreams to reveal what we don't consciously see and to alert us to areas of potential growth.

Our dream animals participate in gender-related narratives in fascinating ways. Considering the basic premise that dream creatures represent our deep instinctual energies, we might begin with two questions: *Is the gender of the dream animal evident? And what is the gender of the owner, which may be literally the person holding the leash?*

Constance Bovier

Lions on Leashes

A man passes in front of me, from right to left with eight adult male lions on leashes (like a dog walker). They all move along rapidly. I'm amazed at the power and potential danger of these animals who could easily all turn on him. Suddenly one lion does turn around and threatens him. But simply by force of character, the man stands his ground and the lion turns back in the direction of their walk as I awaken.

This heavily masculine dream tells me that I have all the resources and competence I need to harness and control the wildest, most powerful of my energies. There are times when I may need to access and employ those capabilities to make my way through life.

To further explore our theme, I offer a low-intensity nightmare that uses a *dream within a dream* structure to convey its message:

Path of Dead Animals

I am sitting in a circle of people discussing dreams when I doze off and dream the following: I am walking along a broad, straight path in a wooded area. It feels oddly enclosed, almost as if it were an indoor setting. A dead horse lies in the path. Its muzzle is pinched and small, not normal for a horse, more like a dinosaur's. As I continue on, I see another dead horse and then more animal carcasses – a mule, then a dog or two – all lying along the path, neglected and decomposing. I know I'm in a man's territory and he's likely very dangerous if he is so callous about animals. I reach a gate where I can get out of this space. I unlock it and am about to open the gate when I sense an even greater danger beyond that enclosed area than what I felt along the path, so I leave the gate shut and retreat.

At this point, I "awaken" back into the first "frame" setting. Sitting in the circle I write this dream into my journal. During the group discussion, I say that people seem to think I always have "nice" dreams, so I begin telling them this one. A man sitting across from me seems the most important person there, someone with whom I should talk more about this dream afterward.

Long before this dream, my spiritual director had gently observed that it appeared difficult for me to remain with my feelings; I typically move quickly from experiencing them to intellectualizing them. I believe this dream's format illustrates that tendency. Here my unconscious creates the security of a dream group within the dream where I can doze off, experience the core message and then immediately process the disturbing awareness after I awaken – all of which allows me to maintain my preferred distance from the troubling feeling content.

So, what is the message here? My introversion places me in an enclosed space, though ostensibly outdoors. While the path ahead is straight and direct, it's littered with dead, decomposing instincts. The powerful horse, the hard-working (albeit stubborn) mule, the loyal dog – while all may have been an active part of the past, they've been too long ignored and left to die. The first horse's narrow, desiccated muzzle suggests that I've lost communication with the energies of my deeper Self, and the "dinosaur" descriptor suggests that this situation has existed for a long while.

Equally distressing, this is *animus* territory – the domain of an unhealthy, uncaring off-screen aspect of my psyche who simply ignores the creatures that lie there moldering. I feel a strange ambivalence about this woods-enclosed space and, when I attempt to exit, I sense even greater danger beyond the gate. Is this the burial ground, the body dump if you will, for all that I have neglected within? How much power have I been relinquishing to my *animus*?

I see an important clue to meaning in the end when my dream ego wakes into the dream frame. I instinctively know the man present in the group is the essential one for me to talk with. My psyche is telling me it will be a *man* who can help me sort out my long-standing imbalance between my masculine/feminine energies and my instincts.

❦

The gender theme couples with a restraint motif in the following dream. My daughter had just spent a day at the Gulf of Mexico, playing in the Galveston surf with her beloved dog, Spirit, then dreamed this:

The Captive Marlin
Kelly Bovier Stearman

I see a man who has a marlin tied up to his boat. He unties the marlin's line and swims away behind the fish, letting it think it is free. They swim down to the bottom of the water in the coastal shelf area. Then the man yanks the line and swims back to the boat, dragging the marlin with him. He re-hooks the line to the boat, leaving the marlin in the water but still tied up, as if he intends to drive the boat onward.

I look deep into the marlin's eyes. It isn't restless or fighting, as if this were a routine that has happened before many times. I reach out and stroke the marlin under its chin for a long time. We seem to have a connection of love like it knows I want to help, yet I can't override its captor. It lets me rub its side as far as my arm will reach.

The marlin seems to have a nose like my golden retriever Spirit, and yet it fully looks like a marlin with its long, pointed bill.

❦

The marlin is a powerful fighter, coveted by deep-sea fishermen. Yet this dream shows the formidable billfish captured, allowed to think it is swimming free when it's actually on a line, reeled back in repeatedly and kept imprisoned against the side of the boat. The dreamer's ego recognizes a long-standing pattern – go just so far, but no farther. She also recognizes the persistent masculine entrapment of her deeply spiritual energy.

Kelly relishes her soul connection through eye contact and touching her sea creature. The dream's weirdly illogical closing image – seeing her dog Spirit's nose on the fish – points to the involvement of the Holy Spirit as a dependable presence in an ongoing relationship that she might forge with this amazing sea creature energy.

What might happen if Kelly reentered this dream to confront the boat driver, rather than accept his being in charge of what goes on within her? What might she say to him about her claim to this magnificent billfish? How might she release the marlin, her own spirit, to swim free and deep with her, around her, within her?

This chapter would fall short without the gender-related dream of a male dreamer. Here we examine a vibrant dream from Steve Wilkerson whose *Engaging Cerberus* appears in *Diamonds in the Details*:

Wild Things
Steve Wilkerson

Arriving home I enter a room with no windows and find that my mother has arranged to keep an adult tiger there. I see my mother just briefly as she leaves to go somewhere so I don't know why the tiger is there – whether it's to be educational or just a pet.

Then I find myself in the room with the large tiger. I am terrified that it will attack and kill/eat me. It comes up to sniff me but never harms me. The tiger is prevented from leaving the room by three walls and a low fence across part of the room. I'm anxious to leave and as I am making my way out, the tiger easily leaps over the low fence into another adjacent area, where there is another much higher fence. That area, still within the room, contains tall brown grass and some low bushes on a dirt embankment.

I leave the room and go into a hall. The lightweight wooden door doesn't close securely behind me, so I'm concerned that the tiger may escape. I look around for twine to wrap around the knob to secure the door so that the tiger cannot get out. In a drawer in the hall, I find a collection of several different brown twines. Some are thick as rope, but I finally find one thin enough to wrap around the knob from the outside to somehow secure the door, so it won't open to let the tiger out.

Both of my daughters come into the house and I explain to them what I am doing. They don't appear concerned, interested, or frightened, as if they think I am overreacting.

Then while I'm in the hallway, I hear a noise. I'm not sure if it's coming from the room with the tiger or another one. I gently push open a door and I see a large lion just inside on the floor. I close the door. I am very concerned lest the lion get loose, leave the house and injure or even kill someone.

As it was apparently my mother who was responsible for getting the lion—I no longer have the tiger in mind—I realize that we could be sued for any damages the lion might create. I wonder if somehow our home owner's insurance will cover this.

Steve arrives home (enters his psyche) as the adventure begins. The tiger's domain is first an ordinary size room, then morphs to include a space about one-third the size of a football field as a new dimension of psyche opens up. "I'm no longer in a civilized, predictable room," said Steve, "but beginning to get into nature. The tiger first seems confined, but when he jumps over the fence and is outside, although we're still inside the room, it's now wild."

Steve is a self-identified INTP on the Myers-Briggs Type Indicator[1] and a five, the observer personality, on the Enneagram[2]. "So I'm a rational thinker and I dwell in my head much too often. This dream is trying to tell me to start recognizing my emotions and body sensations."

In processing his dream, Steve borrowed one of Freud's techniques. "I've read everything Freud wrote about dreams and the words used in dreams were very important to him – not so much their literal meanings but what other words might sound like them." Steve embarked on productive word association relating to the especially resonant word *twine* and found a great deal of ambivalence and contrast. "*To whine* is what a baby does when it wants something," he said. "Although I want the instinctual energy the tiger represents, I'm not quite ready to deal with it yet." So he uses the twine *to wind* around the knob to protect himself from instinctual energy. Looking at other words within *twine* revealed *twin*, which Steve saw as the other part of himself, "my Self, my personal unconscious." He also saw *wine*, both a Christian sacrament and a substance that can temporarily numb feelings and decrease inhibitions. "In wine, there's truth," he said.

Other associations focused on the material itself. "Twine is a coarse type of string and I sometimes *string along* a dream in a superficial fashion," said Steve. Significantly twine is not a refined material but rather primitive, more natural – a fitting association with the natural setting that manifested within the tiger's realm. In waking life, Steve actually has a collection of twine. "One of the shortcomings of the Enneagram five is avarice," he said laughingly. "And I keep my twine collection in the basement, my unconscious." He also noted ambivalence in using twine when a hammer and nails might have been more realistic tools. Why this half-hearted effort? he mused. As uncomfortable as Steve's ego is in this setting with its unknown rooms and disquieting contents, at least some part of him is tentatively ready to confront what is there.

The feminine reigns supreme in this dream. "In terms of *anima*, my mom and my daughters embody both the middle-aged and youthful energy. And it was my mom who got the tiger and lion and put them there." A droll connection: Steve's mother was his high school biology teacher, so the possibility of her obtaining two wild creatures for educational purposes makes perfectly good sense in Steve's dream world.

"My daughters, who are young adults in the dream, are not afraid. The hallway where I meet them is a place of transition, a passage into a new way of feeling, knowing, thinking." Although Steve often felt protective of his girls as they grew up, that isn't the case in the dream at all. "I'm the one who is apprehensive. Even though they're my daughters, they are independent and unconcerned, providing me with protection, confidence and security."

Regarding the dream creatures, Steve's strongest associations come from his grade school years. Growing up as a missionary kid in Taiwan, he didn't have television until the family moved back to North Carolina when he was in the fourth grade. From that era's commercials, he remembers Tony the Tiger, the ESSO mascot, putting energy in the gas tank. And he was strongly affected by the lion Aslan (Christ) in *The Chronicles of Narnia* by C. S. Lewis. "I read that series in grade school and have been taken by the lion since then." While there are numerous Biblical references to lions, Steve noticed another layer of ambivalence in the similarity between *lion* and *lying* down or prevarication. "Sometimes I prevaricate in order to hide from things," he said, which is illustrated in his avoiding the tiger and quickly backing out of the room with the lion.

At the dream's end, Steve's ego makes one final effort to exert itself. He wonders if he is adequately insured to cover any damage that might be caused in the outer world if his creature energies get loose. "My concern about liability coverage is all about rational control," he said. "I'm trying to get back into avoiding my instinctual energy and emotions that are there waiting to be discovered and experienced."

Steve is hardly new to work with the masculine and feminine aspects of the psyche. In his dream leader training at the Haden Institute a decade ago, he delved deeply into this area. He holds this dream as an invitation to re-integration. While the dream concludes with the tiger's and lion's doors closed, he knows he can reopen those doors when he chooses to do so. "My *anima* has the ability to help me make the transition from my intellect into the life of the instincts."

Our final dream about masculine-feminine tension shows once more that a creature needn't be present in living form to convey its energy to the dreamer:

Creative Possibilities

I'm in an activity building in a retreat center. I see a large whiteboard on the right wall that I envision as a place where my group can install their creative works. A man who's in charge of this space (a waking life friend with a powerful personality) comes in, and as I just begin telling him my idea, he draws a large upsweeping triangular shape on the board that he says can be mine to use with my group. I happily imagine the many small pieces of art we can place within those boundaries.

Then a confident, dark-haired woman enters and walks to a whiteboard on the left wall. There she draws a beautifully artistic group of horses, all running to the left. She has no concern at all that her art will eventually be erased from the board.

I'm excited about all the creative possibilities in this place.

Surprisingly this dream came at a time when I was seeing multiple oncologists to determine the best course of treatment for my lung cancer diagnosis. Yet it pulsed with creative energy and left me vibrating with excitement as I awoke.

The dream begins hopefully. Then my ego docilely accepts the boundaries drawn by my overpowering masculine energy (projected onto a friend). The upsweeping shape, artistic and flowing as it is, nevertheless imposes limits. I am disappointingly willing, and apparently content, to remain small as I imagine how much creativity will fit into that defined area.

But one of my feminine personality fragments saves the day! She sweeps in, pays no attention to the man or to me, and boldly produces something of beauty and power. These are no plodding horses for hire. These free-running horses, even though they're drawings, convey unconstrained energy available in my own deep psyche. They've come to illustrate (literally) how I might draw new boldness into my waking life.

Pondering this dream today, I know that my powerful masculine energy might return again to re-exert control and that the beautiful wild horses drawn by my feminine could sink out of sight (erased from the whiteboard) if ignored. It is my choice, as my Self gains confidence, to claim the freedom and creativity of this dream in a space that is truly mine.

Pause

*How have you noticed and experienced gender in your dreams?
How do your dream animals help reveal
issues of conflict and imbalance?*

Composite Creatures

We learn from materials science that composite materials result when two or more distinct components, each with its own characteristics, are combined to create a new substance with properties superior to those of the original components.

Britannica

Inspired by a gifted geology professor in college, I've long been beguiled by rocks and minerals, especially composite and conglomerate specimens formed by dynamic earth processes. This powerful allure of co-mingled natural elements seems mirrored in my fascination with the mergers of dissimilar living creatures in our dreams.

One afternoon adventure on the internet led me to some remarkable two-centuries-old paintings from India in which unknown Hindu artists fused all manner of creatures (and humans) to form elephants, camels and other animals. Writing about these paintings, contemporary artist Ruthie V. said, "I read that they're about interrelatedness of all beings. I'm not sure about the spiritual message, but it looks like people had fun making them."[1]

If your personal theology includes humor, you might think of the Dream Maker having good fun in creating at least some of our hybrid animals. We might also view this phenomenon as the psyche's economy in conflating the characteristics of two or more creatures to more efficiently express ideas. However or whyever these surprises emerge, I agree with the notion that composite animals are about the interrelatedness of all beings or, at the very least, the interrelatedness of energies within the dreamer. Unlike the chimera of mythology and other composite creatures meant to awe or terrify entire communities or cultures, our dream chimeras are personal to us and, as such, certainly warrant consideration.

Over the years my psyche has cobbled together several versions of cats and birds. I've enjoyed beautiful dream cats with feathers growing amidst their fur. And I've marveled at a group of furry, cat-shaped baby birds walking about on the ground, knowing that these cat-birds would morph eventually into smoothly feathered adult birds capable of taking flight.

The following dream introduced a quite different creature bringing a poignant message:

The SheepDog

I'm on a large flat rooftop where I see several dogs wandering about, all different in appearance and breed. A man roaming about with the dogs is loving and encouraging to them. One is a SheepDog, literally. It's puffy white with a dark muzzle – a dog that is also a sheep.

As I watch, it limps away from the dumpster with a morsel of something in its mouth and lies down wearily. The man, the shepherd, comes over and speaks gently, encouraging the big SheepDog to rise and come with him and the others. But this beautiful SheepDog is lying down to rest and to die.

I recognize the man on the rooftop as Jesus. Alternately called the Lamb of God and the Good Shepherd, Jesus is both the sacrificial lamb who is ultimately the Savior of humankind and the firm and loving shepherd who protects us from harm and seeks us when we wander. Likewise, the SheepDog comingles one of the shepherd's charges with a valued canine workmate. I was bemused and deeply stirred by this amalgam of associations.

The setting is reminiscent of Biblical stories where families sometimes ate and slept on their flat roofs in the hot desert climate. In my dreams, higher levels in buildings always point to a spiritual meaning. Here the presence of a dumpster signifies that I should be letting go of something – probably the clutter of my surroundings and my inner world. It also suggests that the debris of my past may already be contained there, situated on the rooftop where I am reaching up toward higher spiritual awareness.

I identify strongly with the SheepDog and feel sad that he must select some part of my psychic discards to eat. This instinctual energy seems worn out. Is it time for me to release this part of myself that is somehow too closely aligned to my past? Is it time for the other energies (the other dogs) to continue onward with the guidance and protection of the holy masculine?

Years later, this dream continues to hold special sweet energy for me.

Next, we explore a dream of composite creatures that appeared during a time of major transition in the dreamer's life. We will see how the animals, embedded in a much longer narrative, help this dreamer look toward her future:

Muddy Dog & Rafter Creatures
Elizabeth J.

I am in my home, an unfamiliar house, when Melissa shows up with a dog and a strange man. They have been traveling together and will spend one night with me. The dog is unruly and Melissa doesn't seem to have any control over it. It's unleashed and running around in the yard. I go to the side of the house and discover Melissa left a hose running—there's camping debris and a big mud hole. The dog runs over to the mud hole and rolls around getting all muddy. I tell Melissa she needs to clean up all of the debris and please don't let the muddy dog into the house.

Later we are inside and the dog is sleeping on a bed. Melissa asks me not to tell her mother about the visit; I promise her I will not tell.

Scene change: I am in a laundry room that is located in a bedroom of the second story of my ex-husband Mickey's house. He is not there as he has been traveling for a very long time. I see spider webs all over everything. The washing machine is lying on its side and the dryer is covered with dirt. I look up and see that some small creatures are making a nest in the rafters. Their presence startles me—they are unexpected. They look like tiny dogs with monkey heads; one is white and the other is gray. I notice that they do not have wings and cannot fly down at me. They seem busy with their nest and are not looking at me, so I am not afraid of them and will leave them alone.

Then Mickey comes into the room and says he wants a new house as this one is old and needs to be remodeled. I tell him I feel the same way about my own house although my washer and dryer are clean.

For Elizabeth, this dream had much to say about her current situation. "I'm in a healing phase of my life and at a crossroads, shifting from retirement into a new vocation as a spiritual director and considering relocation." During recent years many of her sustaining relationships and life structures had fallen away. The death of her only sibling was followed by her forced retirement when her management position was eliminated. Then after caretaking both parents for several years before their deaths, her own deteriorated health demanded she resign from a board presidency that had been intellectually and relationally stimulating. Finally, a gym that had been like a second home and the source of many friendships closed its doors. While several close relationships remain, she concluded, "I've suffered a lot of loss and there is now a vacuum in my life with my community and support network diminished greatly."

Within this context, she processed her dream. "In the first part of the dream, I am in a house on the first floor which feels like the lower part of my psyche. My dog energy seems unrefined and out of control (unruly and unleashed)." The dog's owner, Melissa, is the daring, fun and creative daughter of Elizabeth's best friend and she (an unpredictable personality fragment) and her dog, as the source of the mud and debris outside, reflect the chaos and mess of the dreamer's external life. "As the dream progresses, the dog (now clean and dry) enters my house (my inner world/psyche) and is sleeping on the bed—an indication that some of my discordant emotional energy and fear is now tamed, quieted and settling down."

In the second part of the dream, Elizabeth is in a laundry area of a bedroom on the second floor of a house. The bedroom is unfinished (not ready to be a place of rest) with bare rafters extending up high. The second floor and the high raftered ceiling "indicate movement to a higher and perhaps more evolved or refined level in my psyche." Notice that this house belongs to her ex-husband (material from her past) whom she describes as an intelligent, fun individual. Like Melissa, he's been traveling. Perhaps these two aspects of psyche, previously absent, have returned to be more available to the dreamer ... if she wishes.

Much neglect is evident here with the spider webs, the dirty dryer and the washing machine lying on its side. "This suggests negative fears and beliefs surrounding many of my recent experiences," Elizabeth said. "I seem overwhelmed and not sure of my next step to move forward. I used to trust life but feel I have become paranoid over the last years. I have grief that needs to be healed—so this part of me needs cleaning up."

Then Elizabeth looks upward. "The rafter creatures are a big surprise and don't seem to fit in this dreary room that's in chaos. At first, I'm startled but they are not harmful (no wings to fly down and attack)." The dog-like creatures, Chihuahua in size, have big eyes and small ears. "There is something human-like in their faces – a cuteness, like small monkeys. They seem sweet, calm and busy. They work together cooperatively, making no sounds, building a little straw nest like a bird's. They know their purpose and patiently, persistently work on their little home."

What might these small composite creatures be offering Elizabeth? Perhaps at this point in her life, the rambunctious big dog energy of the opening needs to be left asleep for a while. Such intensity isn't what's needed at this point in her journey. Her small composite creatures introduce several contrasting elements. They combine the familiar canine traits of loyalty and lifelong companionship with the human-like primate intelligence of sweet-natured, light-hearted monkeys. Elizabeth added, "While dogs are domesticated, monkeys always retain their wild nature. So this seems like a blending of my wild, maybe more authentic, nature with the more civilized part of me – two archetypes merging together."

Her rafter creatures also display contrasting colors: one is white, the other gray. While gray suggests a more ambivalent, uncommitted stance, white often points to new beginnings and transformation, here perhaps signifying a lofty (spiritual) level of their promising message of things to come.

At the end of the dream, Mickey's comment underscores that this house (life/psyche) is old and needs remodeling to be livable. At the same time, Elizabeth knows that she has a clean washer and dryer in her own home that will enable her to clean up and begin afresh. She also knows that her rafter creatures are healthy and fertile and modeling how to diligently create a new home – with great promise for her future.

"I feel these little creatures also represent my head and heart working together—a marriage of intellect and intuition," said Elizabeth. "And I feel they represent a new vision for my life that is slowly forming. For now, it is perhaps just a small feeling or impulse, not yet a physical reality, but as time unfolds, my new life will be quietly born."

Finally, let's savor a brief encounter with an exquisite composite creature who appeared to a long-time dreamworker:

Kitten-Headed Butterfly
Lane Turner Norton

I see an incredibly large butterfly, with a wingspan of perhaps three feet across. Its wings are made of jewels and gems of many colors and shapes. I am riveted, unable to tear my eyes from all the colors, shapes and forms. There are symbols formed from enamel, gold and pearls, and tiny cameos, as well as stones of every color and value all connected by links of golden chain.

I look away for a moment and, when I look back, the body and head of the insect have been transformed into that of a sleeping, gray tabby kitten. Again, I am transfixed with the wonder and joy that this brings me.

♥

This breathtaking image delighted the dreamer, who held it for many months before taking it to her dream group. Through that process, Lane said, "What came into more and more prominence was the awe and wonder I felt, *and still feel,* and the numinous quality of the images."

Her first associations upon awakening from this dream centered on the jeweled butterfly. "Its wings looked as though they were encrusted with slides from a Victorian slide bracelet," she said. "In waking life I have only seen one, which I believe belonged to my mother-in-law." In such jewelry, the individual "slides" are beautifully decorative little works of art in themselves, suggesting great variety and diversity in this enormous dream butterfly.

"When I awoke, I was also reminded of Chessie, the sleeping kitten in the logo of the Chesapeake & Ohio Railway System. Their slogan was *Sleep Like a Kitten,*" said Lane. "I adore cats, and in my 67 years have never been long without one in my life and my home. I love them for their beauty and grace, their independence, their affection, and the mystery they personify, being able to walk freely between the worlds wild and domestic. Cats see in the dark and into the unconscious." Reflecting on the cat in mythology, she relates strongly to the image of the Minoan snake goddess with bared breasts, serpents in both hands and a cat perched on her head – a precursor to Athena, originally honored as a goddess of wisdom.

As Lane experienced with this dream, processing may occur in bursts over time. After months of honoring her *Kitten-Headed Butterfly*, she suddenly recalled something from years before. "I was once fascinated by microscopic photos of the scales on butterflies' wings. I Googled those images and, though none of them were exactly like my dream image, I remember that their iridescence and colors were astoundingly beautiful."

Lane continues to hold her stunning dream image as both confirmation and invitation. "I believe that the Dream Maker was asking me to look deeply into the beauty and wonder in the natural world. Rather than being repulsed or frightened by gargantuan insect features, I'm offered the transformational wonder of the micro-world coupled with the comfort and peace of a sleeping kitten. I give thanks to the Divine for the transformational joy, and the peace-giving nature of this dream."

In closing, Lane added, "Wonder and peace are tools that are so very necessary if we are to navigate our way through a world increasingly fraught with fear and isolation."

As these dreams have shown, there's much we can learn from our most unlikely creatures. But before we leave the subject of composite animals, I invite you to turn to the next chapter, to meet a hybrid nightmare beast that confounded me for many years.

Dream Animal Wisdom

Pause

*What creature energies have merged in your dreams?
How might you honor each aspect of your creature
as your dream releases its wisdom?*

MoleCat's Revelation

It is often difficult to understand fully what a dream is trying to do.... The dream may end badly or contain no closure or concluding direction. When faced with this situation, the dream can still be used as a platform to create a possible new metaphor for closure. You can use a form of what Jung called Active Imagination or dream reentry and spontaneous visualization to complete the dream.

Robert Hoss

This is the story of MoleCat, an appalling creature who burst from my unconscious in a shocking nightmare in 2006. I'd gone to bed blithely anticipating a peaceful night. I was, after all, in the serene setting of a prayer retreat. Instead, I received a series of nightmares that included a collapsing ceiling in my house, the threat of a serial rapist, the inability to find my car, my fruitless struggle to report the missing car problem and finally escaping the danger of a fire that started in a general store.

It was not my best night in the dream world!

Out of that chaos emerged MoleCat in a formidable dream that inscribed every detail into my memory and trailed its haunting effects through subsequent years. I attended to this Big Dream the best I could at the time, filling the margins of my journal pages with diligent processing notes. While I uncovered many useful insights, the nature and purpose of the composite creature central to my dream continued to elude me for a long time.

Here is the dream:

MoleCat and the Puppy

I am in a tight outdoor street setting, a winding, cramped medieval-like street where some men are restraining a large beast, MoleCat, that is clearly out for blood. The creature is solid and stocky, with short, stiff brown hair and a red pointy muzzle and feet. It is focused on the building across the narrow street where a happy, innocent, floppy-eared brown puppy is looking out the window, eagerly observing the scene, oblivious to the danger. It's clear to me that the men are baiting MoleCat and intend to let the puppy out and watch this creature kill it for sport. I'm horrified and I know that I can't stop it.

I retreat into the building to my left where I find myself in a small bedroom with a TV. I'm nearing panic as I try to turn on the TV to drown out what I know will be awful noises. But there are far too many buttons on the TV and I can't find the power switch. When I finally get the TV on, I can hear an animal crying outside.

I was appalled. Even now, I pause for a moment after reading this dream. Yet the Dream Maker knew I was ready at that specific point in my life for the upswell of dark material that poured into consciousness.

The compressed setting of this dream with its narrow, winding medieval street, tells me I'm dealing with some old material. When my fearful ego drives me to seek refuge in a building bordering the street, I enter the small rented room where my first husband had lived during his final years when his life had become constricted by the grip of alcoholism. My sadness at that realization is subsumed by anguish over the situation outside.

My desperation to get the TV going is the childish behavior of plugging my ears and singing *la-la-la* to cover up something I don't want to hear – for an adult, a cowardly escape from a situation too frightening to handle. I also recognize that the unknown men restraining MoleCat embody my controlling nature at its worst.

The hog-size MoleCat, with its stiff brown hair, pointy snout, small red eyes and powerful killing instinct, expresses an array of animal traits that I find alarming and repulsive. Together the men and the grotesque MoleCat represent parts of me that are poised to overpower and vanquish joy – the happiness showcased in the window, the puppy eagerly bouncing against the glass barrier, longing to burst outside for some fun.

I've long admitted to an under-developed sense of play. Typically, my moments of joy are neatly contained, described rather than expressed, so I won't embarrass myself by appearing out of control. In this dream, the jubilant puppy exudes the unapologetic goofiness that makes dogs so funny and lovable – behavior I would *never* deliberately allow in myself. (No wonder I'm a cat person; while a cat may make a demented dash throughout the house, she'll rarely admit that it was *she* who'd just played the fool for all to see.)

For years I believed this dream showed me the darkest aspect of my shadow, my hidden killer instinct, turned against bright shadow, my unabashedly joyful self. Meanwhile, I gleaned practical wisdom by acknowledging that my avoidance of the street scene reflects my predisposition to withdraw from life's difficulties. Applying this lesson in my waking life, I began to grapple intentionally with personal challenges and family responsibilities in a more mature, pro-active way.

Yet despite my processing, my life applications and an occasional re-reading during the intervening years, this dream never yielded an answer to the central question: *Who and what is MoleCat?* The question became impossible to continue sidestepping as I began envisioning this book. MoleCat and I had unfinished business.

This perplexing dream rushed to the forefront one morning at the neighborhood park. After feeding the community cats and stowing my supplies in my car, I set off on my fitness walk. I don't recall any conscious preparation. It simply was time to begin learning the truth about my strange composite creature with the incomprehensible name.

So I re-entered my dream as I walked:

Active Imagination #1

I am walking along the narrow, twisting little street and I approach the scene where I see a lone man and MoleCat. This time I refuse to be intimidated by my powerful animus. Instead, I confront MoleCat itself as it strains toward the puppy behind the window. I begin speaking gently, much as I'd just done with the feral cats at their feeding station. "It's alright," I tell MoleCat. "You don't need to do this. You don't need to kill anything. It's okay. You'll be okay."

As I continue soothing the fierce creature, MoleCat begins shrinking in size, then deflates, until it is small enough that the man who'd been restraining it with a chain, picks it up like a sheet of paper, folds it, puts it in his pocket and then he too disappears.

Alone now, I turn and raise the window to free the little brown puppy. It leaps out and into my arms, exuberantly squirming, yipping and slobbering me with kisses. I notice that the street is no longer as narrow as it had been. And the puppy is no longer small. As I place the growing dog on the ground to my right, we begin walking away on an ever-broadening street. With every step the dog grows larger until I can place my hand easily on his head as we walk onward together.

My nightmare had unquestionably deserved a new ending and this one released many feelings. As I wrote down my newly imagined conclusion, it triggered memories of the grief work I'd done following the memorial service for my first husband after his passing. In revisiting this dream scene and the narrow little street, it felt right and appropriate to walk past his former little rented room. Those were not my walls to live within. And I was no longer the young woman whose efforts at control made no difference in my husband's personal struggle with alcoholism. It was time to walk away from that part of my past.

I also saw from this active imagination that I had courage enough to confront whatever lies within. Like a child turning her nightmare beast into a teddy bear, I was able to speak to MoleCat, a subterranean part of myself now out in the open. Confronted, it responded by shrinking, deflating and becoming "a paper tiger," no threat at all to a healthy psyche.

In facing the exuberant puppy (a long-neglected part of myself) as it leaped against the window, I took a new step toward adventure. Overwhelmed at first by the happy-dog energy, I was willing and open to possibilities. As I strode forth into the future, the jubilant puppy became a more mature companion, right at my side, moving forward with me.

Initially, after this experience, I felt celebratory about what had happened – until I noticed an unsettled feeling about the way the scene had played out. Specifically, I was uneasy with how MoleCat had shrunken, deflated and flattened to the point that the male handler was able to pick up the creature, fold it up like a piece of paper, pocket it and disappear. It felt too facile, too convenient, like the contrived *deus ex machina*, god from the machine, that swooped in to solve the conflict in ancient Greek dramas. Finally, I grasped that I was feeling great compassion toward MoleCat and whatever the creature represented. I simply couldn't bear its being disposed of in such an offhand way. Besides that, without the chance for dialog, I *still* didn't know who or what MoleCat was and what it had come to show me in the first place.

By now, it was clear that I'd encountered archetypal energy, that MoleCat was something greater than a simple (though hybrid) living creature. As I considered another time of active imagination, I felt anxious. But I couldn't allow this intense, straining energy to simply dwindle and end up in someone's pocket. I also realized that my resistance to the first new ending was at least partly due to its leaving my dominant masculine energy in charge. It was he, after all, who had tucked MoleCat away and departed. And that *certainly* didn't feel right.

So I ventured into my dream again:

Active Imagination #2

I am back in the street and I see the man in charge who now stands with his hands on his hips grinning at me.

"I want to see MoleCat again," I say.

"You sure?" he asks, still grinning.

"Yes. I want to see it again."

He reaches into his pocket and pulls out the paper. "Better get ready!"

He flings the paper out onto the ground between us and it erupts into the MoleCat creature, bigger than before, now about the size of a bear. It rushes up to me and roars in my face, its pointy red muzzle opening to reveal sharp teeth and a rush of fetid breath.

I quake with fear and I want to scream and run. But I stand my ground. I remind myself that this is my own imaginary material and I refuse to be bullied by any of the characters!

I ask MoleCat, "Can we talk? Please talk to me. What can we do to learn about each other?"

MoleCat chokes on a growl and looks at me, puzzled. It sits back on its haunches and stares at me. "You think that hiding accomplishes anything?"

"Well, I'm afraid of you and what you can do."

"It's you who let me get this big," MoleCat says, "by staying all neat and together on the outside to impress everybody. I eat and grow on stuffed emotions, you know. I love resentments, disappointments, all the stuff you don't know what to do with in your waking life."

MoleCat glares at me then gets up, turns his back and goes to stand beside the man who is still grinning at me. A leash dangles from the man's hand, unused.

Dream Animal Wisdom

Well, that felt awful, especially what MoleCat said. It seemed true all right, but still unfinished and unsatisfying. The masculine energy in this encounter is strong as ever and, what's more, he's now smug and sarcastic. By now, I understand that MoleCat is a deep energy that I absolutely *must* integrate if I am to consider myself healed. Something in me knows that MoleCat must be released, reclaimed and redeemed by the feminine.

Holding this awareness, on another day, I revisited the dream once again:

Active Imagination #3

I walk along the street toward MoleCat and the man restraining it. The puppy remains safely behind the window of the building on my right. As I approach them, MoleCat stops straining at its leash and sits on its haunches. The man and I look at one another.

"I'll take it from here," I tell him.

Surprisingly, he doesn't resist but offers me the leash.

"I don't need that."

"Okay. Have it your way." He removes the leash from MoleCat and, carrying it with him, disappears.

MoleCat looks at me. After a moment, he stands up, seems to rock a bit on its feet, bracing for what? An attack?

"I'm back," I say. "I'm tired of being fearful and avoiding tough things. I believe you are everything that I've pushed down rather than facing up to what is."

No answer.

I just can't stop at this unfinished point. "What can we do about this?"

MoleCat sits again and looks downward.

I approach slowly and stand beside him. I place my arm across his back. I'm surprised that what looked like stiff, wiry hair is actually soft. MoleCat turns his head and looks up at me with a small noise.

We stand there for a long moment, then something amazing begins to happen. MoleCat transforms into two distinct creatures, both much smaller in size than the huge composite creature. A small brown mole turns away and scurries off to burrow back underground where it belongs.

The other creature, a large golden cat, remains with me. She rumbles a greeting deep in her chest. She blinks her great golden eyes at me and sits, waiting.

I look at the building where the puppy has been sitting quietly inside the window, watching what's been taking place. I open the door and the puppy comes out. He and the cat gaze at each other.

"Come on then," I say. "Both of you."

They fall into step with me and we turn to walk away down the avenue that has straightened and broadened from the narrow medieval street. I'm aware of the sinuous grace of the cat at my left and I hear the soft panting of the dog that has grown up at my right side.

I feel protected, energized and emboldened as I emerge from the tight restrictions and constraints of apprehensive living. No longer are any vital aspects of myself left buried away or deformed and unfulfilled.

The three, no, the four of us are all finally free.

I wept. After years of holding this Big Dream, I'd finally met the energies that had been compressed by my psyche into a ravening beast. I now understood that the archetypal Cat, the Great Feminine, had been cast into the subterranean darkness of my psyche in mole-like fashion due to my inability to comprehend her true nature. Stuffed and repressed throughout my adult life, this deep energy burrowed up and out like a mutated beast with barely restrained fury, ready for blood, ready to vanquish any joyful energy that had been allowed to live in the light. MoleCat had paid the price, embodying all the powerful energy my ego had kept out of sight, literally buried underground.

Dream Animal Wisdom

I believe my experience confirms what Robert Johnson meant in saying that it is the dreamer who must bring the "ethical, humane, and practical elements" into active imagination.[1] Once confronted and disarmed with compassion, MoleCat transformed into the powerful golden Cat, releasing the poor burrowing mole from its conscripted service to a murderous part of my shadow to return freely to the part of the earth where it belonged.

Following my active imagination work, I turned to a SoulCollage card I'd made some months earlier. There, beside an arched threshold to the future, stands a gleaming Golden Cat as sentry. Today this Golden Cat helps me appreciate how all my domestic cats – dreamed and real, feral and tame – have been advising and tending me over all the intervening years until I was able to welcome and integrate this deeper reality.

How grateful I am to the amazing creature, MoleCat, for upending my self-perceptions, and to the little mole itself, for the service it performed until I was ready to see the light. Now that I have met my Golden Cat and loyal new canine companion, perhaps we might even encounter some of my other cats now living in the expanded realm of my interior landscape, roaming free.

Pause

What perplexing dream creature continues
pulsing energy into your current life?
How might you revisit your dream animal in active imagination?

Life, Death and Resurrection

What emerges in dreams is [often] unknown, out of the ego's control,
counter to the aims of the ego, and generally requires
the ego to give in (symbolically die) ....
Material or issues we have suppressed because we
don't want to deal with them might emerge
as dead things, as fragments of self that have been
"dead" to our conscious persona
that the ego does not want to confront.

Robert Hoss

In his deep-reaching book, *The Universal Christ*, Richard Rohr writes of "the universal pattern of growth and healing through loss and renewal. This universal pattern is the way that life perpetuates itself in ever-new forms – ironically, through various kinds of death."[1] Rohr goes on to point out that scientists seem to understand the pattern better than the churches which have tended to limit the pattern of death and resurrection to the life of Jesus. I would add that dreamworkers join the scientists in this realization.

Maybe you remember the first time a dream group or mentor helped you understand that your ghastly dream about death was, at its core, a message of renewal and that death in dreams generally constitutes one of our most instructive dream metaphors. We eventually learn to accept, even welcome, dreams that would have been shocking to us in our pre-dreamwork pasts.

For instance:

Where the Bodies are Buried

I am walking alongside a long, rectangular derelict building on my right. I turn left and continue along an area of scrubby underbrush. I am following Joe, but we don't interact. Then I see

Joe in an area where he is excavating a group of human skeletons. I'm startled at one skull that seems unusually large. I see many other bones and skulls and I know that the town is responsible for killing and burying these people here.

Suddenly a medium-sized skeleton dog, standing beside me to my right, starts barking at me. I'm really surprised at that!

❣

At the time of this dream, I was engrossed in the TV drama, *The Man in the High Castle*[2], and I'd just viewed an episode in which Joe, an alarmingly dutiful Nazi, buried victims in a mass grave. Here, he is digging up bodies – unearthing something that it's time for me to see.

As the dream opens, I recognize that some part of my life has been abandoned (the derelict building). While it may have been suitable at one time, that structure (attitude? worldview? way of being?) is no longer serviceable, no longer where I need to be. So I turn away from it toward my intuitive side.

What part of me is Joe unearthing? The town (the collective) has done away with all of these fragments of myself. Once again, I understand that I've been too much out in the world, emotionally, spiritually, and this is the result. It is up to Joe, a chillingly logical masculine energy, to show me this truth. The skull with its grotesquely oversized brain case stands out starkly. As Joe lifts it up, I see that I've placed far too much value on intelligence, learning, thinking, doing – and look what that has accomplished.

The grand finale (in case I don't comprehend the full significance of the skull) is the skeletal dog barking at me: *Look! Listen! See where your brainpower has gotten you – buried in a ditch. Because of the way you've been living, I'm nothing but an empty skeleton. It's up to you to put some meat on my bones, to reclaim my energy, so I can be useful to you.*

Waking from this dream, my heart went out to this poor dog, crying out to me for reconstitution, for a return to what it should be. More than a shadow from my unconscious, this dog denotes a move toward my heart. It represents a potentially vibrant, sustaining energy that, once enfleshed, can help me continue onward in a more balanced way than how I've been living.

While I hadn't been consciously aware of a need for restoration or renewal until this dream upended my status quo, it's noteworthy that the Dream Maker chose the dog as the appropriate messenger for such critical information.

We see psyche's use of the dog once again in the following dream shared by a spiritual director friend with long experience on the inner journey:

Resurrection
Karen K.

My husband and I have been asked to temporarily watch our friends' dead dog, a medium-sized light chocolate brown mutt or Lab mix. As we observe the dog in our living room, we're surprised to see the dog gradually coming to life. First, it lies there and moves a little, then gradually more, without much effect. Eventually, it comes to vibrant liveliness, barking and wagging its tail. We are excited and we play with the dog. We tell our friends what is happening, but they seem unconcerned, which is confusing to us.

Karen remembers reading this to her dream group and, noticing that she was wearing a light chocolate brown top, suddenly realizing that *she* was the dog in her dream. "I think the dream at one level is about my own resurrection from feeling dead and useless to feeling competent and needed," she said. "It's been a slow, gradual process getting here."

Before this dream, Karen had prayed to see the face of Jesus in her dreams and she feels this was part of this answer: "Jesus and I have both been through resurrection." The dog's mixed-breed presence indicates oneness or unity, underscoring the dual representation of Jesus and herself. The resurrection theme has tremendous energy for Karen, linked with her long interest in healing, her practice of several healing modalities and two new opportunities in her waking life. "Both are surprises since I didn't go looking for either one, but I'd only prayed to be used."

Karen's dream spoke to her on a familial level as well. She and her husband were keeping watch over an adult son at home (the living room setting), who was suffering from depression and working toward a college degree. In her reflection, Karen feels the living room represents the tomb or cave where Jesus lay after his crucifixion and where he (and the dog) come back to life. "A container for the dead becomes the place of awakening," she said. "The place where life is reborn."

Pondering the gift of this dream for herself and her family, Karen said, "Multiple people are experiencing resurrection in this dream and in my waking life. Thinking of our house as a healing place for our son is very helpful to me. We are facilitating his healing, as well as his completing his degree – bringing him to wholeness." It is also a place of healing for Karen as she emerges from her own depression into active participation in life. "I love this!" she said.

Karen's dream group helped her look for God's movement in her life and ways she could choose what is happy, exciting and joyful. Her dream confirmed what was already taking place, allowing her to tend her reawakening deep energy (the dog), to accept that it didn't belong to someone else (the off-screen friends) but to her, and to integrate it into her newly revitalized waking life.

Grief and loss in one's waking life also provide fertile soil for resurrection dreams.

We met Becky O. in previous chapters (*Birds* and *Sea Creatures*), where she was guided and comforted by those creatures during her mother's final illness and her own cancer journey. During the months following her mother's passing, as she said farewell to her beloved dog, Jack, and welcomed her mother's cat, Benji, into her home – she lived in an interim time where nothing had yet regained clarity. "I was in the place that John O'Donohue describes," she said: *The old is not old enough to have died away. The new is still too young to be born.*[3]

Then a tender new animal energy emerged from this pensive time of in-between. Here is Becky's calico kitten trilogy:

Death into New Life
Becky O.

I am in my home cleaning the guest bathroom countertop. I glance into the commode to check its cleanliness. In the water is a small calico kitten. I wonder what it's doing there. Then I notice it's actually underwater with its eyes closed and mouth open. I quickly pick it up, turn it upside down and gently pat it on the back. She begins to heave up water. I take a small towel and, holding her to my chest, begin to rub life back into her. She doesn't make a sound but wiggles closer into the warmth. I am hopeful.

In a place usually associated with flushing away the unwanted, unneeded refuse of the body, lies a tiny near-dead creature, awaiting revival. Notice the setting, a guest bathroom, which is a place in Becky's home (life) where she would not often be. Fortunately, she arrives just in time!

Surprised and pleased by this dream, Becky said, "Noticing and rescuing the kitten feels like an invitation to offer healing care once more. As I hold her close to my heart, we seem to nurture each other." She feels that her season of return from illness and loss is a time of intentional self-care. "Perhaps the multi-colored kitten represents varied opportunities leading me to a new dimension of healing through spiritual direction. I trust and am waiting hopefully."

Contrasting this encounter to her *Caged Birds* dream (*Birds* chapter) and her felt sense that her huge multi-colored bird was finally freed, she meets here a freshly different animal energy. This invitation comes as a tiny, helpless, multi-colored kitten, a creature of the earth, a warm and hopeful new energy to integrate as Becky moves toward a new phase of her life.

Then in the spring of 2020, six weeks into the COVID-19 pandemic, Becky began noticing something new. "Every night my dream screen was filled with gentle swirling colors of blue, almost like an ocean tide pool. It was a calming, assuring place to be, even with all the virus warnings filling the news."

Into this soothing dreamscape came her second kitten dream:

Notice Me!
Becky O.

I am in the swirling blue colors and then in an instant, it all pauses. I look to my left at my kitchen table and six chairs. Under my chair I see the calico kitten, sitting on its haunches, looking unconcerned. Then the gentle swirling begins again.

Ah, I think upon awakening. The kitten's back and she's sitting in a place of honor.

The kitchen is the heartbeat of Becky's home. "It's a gathering place where generosity and hospitality flow," she said. "It's a sacred place where stories are shared, old memories are revisited and new memories are created."

Of the six chairs, the kitten chooses to sit beneath the one where Becky typically sits. While six is the suitable number for Becky's table, that number also suggests domestic harmony, love and abundance. "Maybe the energy of my chair is one of server, integrator, inviter, provider, gatherer and laughter!" she said. The kitten knows to whom she belongs yet seems unimpressed by that "honor", which the dreamer finds "quite comical."

In pondering the significance of the swirling blues, Becky said, "I know it represents God becoming springs of living water for me during these desert times."

Her third kitten dream occurred two months later:

Come Find Me
Becky O.

I'm in a retreat setting on a low back porch. Fall leaves cover the surrounding yard. Children are playing a game, running back and forth, laughing. Curious, I notice the leaves by the porch moving. I reach down and pick up a small pile and as the leaves fall away, I'm left holding a calico kitten. She begins to squirm, so I put her down laughing.

Then another section of leaves begins to move. Once again, I pick up a small pile and this time as the leaves fall away a baby owl flutters its wings. In astonishment, I squeal, "I've always wanted to hold an owl!" Then the owl flutters away, back into the leaves. This sequence repeats several times. It's a delight.

My friend Cindy calls from inside the house, "You need to pack, Becky. It's almost time to leave!"

As I enter the bedroom, I notice my clothes lying in a heap on the floor. A red zip-up velvety flannel robe is on top. Then the robe begins to hop around, and out comes the calico kitten! I try to tell those around me about my unusual morning, but no one is listening. The kids are still playing, Cindy is still packing, and the leaves are still moving.

"Fall has always been my favorite time of year," Becky said. "I love the transition of green leafy trees to stark branches. I walk many miles every fall kicking leaves into the air and laughing as they fly in the wind." So this dream setting is a natural environment for Becky, and her youthful spirit of play abounds. While her inner children happily run about in the background, she's drawn into a game with her instinctive energies.

"Hide and seek was scary for me as a child because we typically played at night when there was the creepy unknown." But here it is morning and the fall leaves are a happily familiar element from which this youthful pair of animals emerge. "In childhood, I would always choose to play with creatures over humans," she said, "so this game of hide and seek is just delightful with fresh energy inviting me to participate in the discovery." The game repeats again and again, as the kitten and the baby owl reinforce their determined emergence into consciousness.

Contrasting this scene with her dreams of vividly colored caged birds and her snowy owl in the *Birds* chapter, she recognizes a distinct shift in energy. This baby owl is a multi-colored brown, a more earthy, "natural" color, to blend in with the trees and the leaves, perhaps to introduce a new kind of wisdom. And the calico kitten, a mixture of white and muted colors, suggests integration and a softer, different sort of energy.

Cindy, a wise spiritual friend with whom Becky attends many retreats, reminds her dreaming self that it's time to pack and depart this place of joyful play. But the kitten seems determined to come along, playing a new game of hide and seek under Becky's comfortable red robe. This kitten is not an energy to be ignored or left behind! The owl, though still outdoors in the moving leaves, may very well fly to join Becky and the kitten later.

Ultimately, in this deeply personal encounter, it doesn't matter that the other parts of the dreamer ignore her story. Becky knows what has happened. And along with the wonderful possibilities of her kitten and baby owl energies, she carries forward the promise underscored by the red robe at the end of the dream – a promise of resurrection into new creativity.

Pause

*How are your dream animals inviting you toward revitalization in your waking life?
What dream creature is entreating: "Please take me with you"?*

Transformations

*In dreams the hero is generally you, your dream-self,
embarking on a transformational journey:
going into the unconscious; meeting, confronting and defeating
our conflicts and fears and integrating our shadow side; and
eventually, after many dreams or dream segments,
being transformed or reborn as a new self with a new attitude.*

Robert Hoss

Houston lies in the migration path of the monarch butterfly, which creates some stunning moments for residents during the fall. A friend at church has regaled our small group with tales and photos of her backyard butterfly nursery and offered guidance to others about choosing butterfly-enticing plants and monitoring the grand metamorphosis from voracious caterpillar to winged creature of beauty and grace. What remarkable amounts of energy a creature must marshal to begin life in one form and transform into something entirely different. What, we wonder, did the Divine Creator have in mind with all of this?

The striking alterations of some insects and amphibians offer us much plenty to ponder. As dreamers, we're invited to grasp the meanings of metamorphosis *for us* in the ways our total-makeover dream creatures bring their unique realities into our dreams. As we'll see in some brief examples and then a longer series, the psyche uses precisely targeted ways to present transformative ideas.

Here is the clever use of an offstage creature to offer a timely message to the dreamer:

Listening to My Inner Voice
Emma Adeline R.

I am being told by someone: "What if you are a butterfly?" I know this is said as a negative, degrading comment meant to exclude and discourage me from doing something. Fear sets in, but I immediately say to myself, "Wait a minute! Butterflies are beautiful and represent transformation and resurrection!" So I dismiss the fear monger and go back to sleep.

Emma Adeline awoke tearfully from her dream that morning. Immersed in difficult situations within her family and her church congregation, she was feeling as if others in her waking life owned her – that she was not merely being taken advantage of, like Cinderella, but that she was fully *owned*, dominated.

While the butterfly itself doesn't actually appear, her butterfly associations center on their delicate, wondrous beauty. But here a voice of authority insinuates something quite different. Emma Adeline hears her negative inner critic implying that she, like a butterfly, is flighty, unsubstantial, inconsistent or unpredictable. Who is this personality fragment who enslaves her, suggesting that she's incapable of handling relationships or confronting challenges in daily living?

This small dream-vision urged Emma Adeline to set aside the fears generated by the disembodied voice, to align instead with the beautiful aspects of her dream creature and to claim the butterfly's transformative energy for herself in her dealings with others in her waking life.

Another unique butterfly message emerged from a brief dream snippet and active imagination of another dreamer:

The Worms
Margie O.

I am standing in front of a group of people who are all facing me. I see what appears to be worms, about the size of my little finger, moving around just under their skin.

Margie dreamed this image the night after her husband returned home from a worrisome lung biopsy and hospitalization. "While he was in intensive care, I was only able to see him for a few minutes every four hours and I had such an empty feeling, knowing the disease that has damaged his lungs can progress to other organs in his body." Her anxiety coalesced into this unsettling dream impression of writhing worms.

The power of this image lingered for months until the couple attended a dream conference where Margie took part in a guided meditation. As she re-entered her dream, she once again faced the persons who had worm-like movement beneath their skin. "I remained with that image until, to my surprise and delight, butterflies emerged from each of the moving places and filled the air all around me."

By the time of this meditation, her husband was receiving medical treatment and her psyche responded by transforming the worry worms (embodied by many parts of her personality) into caterpillars, which then emerged as butterflies of hope. Margie was delighted by this experience. As butterflies filled the air around her, they released all the trapped negative energy of her original dream image.

In a host of synchronicities since that time, Margie has been graced by the gentle visits of a variety of butterflies upon her own skin.

I remember my childhood delight at spotting a jellied mass of frog eggs in the shallows of a pond or stream, later watching the wriggly little tadpoles (I still favor the way *pollywog* rolls over my tongue) who bore little resemblance to the frogs they were destined to become. *Well, let's just grow some lungs and legs, shall we? And while we're at it, let's ditch the tail.*

While butterflies elicit spontaneous ohhhs and ahhhs, frogs generally make me chuckle and grin. In the following odd but instructive dream, I meet a frog who simply keeps on changing. Here, the best word is *transmogrifying*, that great humorous term suggesting magical and bizarre changes, popularized by *Calvin and Hobbes*[1]:

The Two-Headed Frog

I have a pet frog about the size of my hand. I'm disturbed to see a sore on the left side of its face near its mouth. When I see it later, I'm astonished to see that what appeared to be a wound is a new mouth forming. And an eye is beginning to appear above it. I realize that an entirely new head is emerging on the frog! I want to take photos and make notes to document this unusual occurrence.

Then suddenly, I am outdoors in a beach area where a concrete ledge covers an area of rocks and dirt. I am digging out materials from under the ledge with my hands. I'm concerned about undermining and weakening the concrete slab, but I'm thrilled to find specimen after specimen of various minerals. I'm excited and tremendously happy. It's as if I'm finding a treasure that I'd long forgotten.

These two seemingly unrelated dream scenes interweave at a deep level. The startling growth (an entirely new head emerging) includes a new eye (a new perspective) and a new mouth (a new call to self-expression). I don't take time to intellectualize or document the morphing frog phenomenon as my logical self is inclined to do. But comprehending the wondrous development underway is all that's needed to open me up to what's been hidden within for a long time.

I'm led to a threshold (the beach) where I uncover something of great worth that I'd abandoned there long before. During my thirties, I was active in mineral collecting and I still have a few favorite specimens on my shelves. To me, digging up beautiful crystalline minerals is an apt metaphor for finding the Biblical "pearl of great price." I need no special tools beyond my hands to do the task of unearthing treasure that I can carry forward with me into waking life.

Leaving behind my little morphing frog, we move to a life-changing series of frog dreams shared by Tallulah Lyons, one of my earliest dream mentors. The author of two dream books[1] and a long-time dream teacher and facilitator, Tallulah spent many years guiding groups of cancer patients and their families in accessing the healing power of dreams.

It's been more than two decades since Tallulah encountered the creature that was to become her primary animal guide into psychospiritual growth and healing. "My initial encounter with Frog," she said, "was in a dream that shook me to my core."

Saving the Black Boy from Frog Man
Tallulah Lyons

I'm walking down an almost deserted street in a foreign city when I see a shadowy man grab a small black boy and stuff him head-down into a garbage can. Filled with horror, I race forward swinging my pocketbook. I hit the man squarely on the head and knock him unconscious. As he sinks to the ground, his legs slowly transform into frog legs. Terrified, I pull the boy from the garbage by his feet. We run and don't look back, but I know that the man has become a giant frog and that I'll meet him again.

❣

Tallulah remembers that this soul-shaking dream occurred the week before she began her training at the Haden Institute[3] to become a certified dream group facilitator. On the first day, as class members gathered for dream sharing, she found herself in a small group led by the late dreamwork pioneer Jeremy Taylor. Her frog dream was chosen as the focus. "I look back on this experience as the most important turning point in my life," Tallulah said. "As Jeremy and the others projected on my dream, my soul resonated with the new insights that were offered." For the first time, she heard of concepts like shadow work, archetypal experience, and the collective unconscious.

"This dream is an affirmation of my commitment to move into unknown territory (the foreign city) and affirms my growing trust in intuitive action (whacking the man with my purse). It feels like a call to rescue unrecognized and neglected vulnerable parts of myself (the black boy). I also glimpse the certainty that my path will require a transformed relationship with huge, unsavory shadow elements of myself (the frog man)."

In the context of this dream, and through reading Jeremy Taylor's book, *The Living Labyrinth*, Tallulah learned the deep truth contained in the universal fairy tale about the frog that becomes a prince – that to grow, one must embrace and *marry* (integrate) the ugly frog within. From that point onward, she began working with shadow parts of her personality that appeared as disturbing dream characters. "I gradually became less afraid of confronting the unconscious as I experienced a positive transformation of the personified fears."

A year after her *Frog Man* dream, Tallulah was deeply impacted by the following synchronicity as her waking experience suddenly connected with her ongoing inner work:

Embracing the Bullfrog
Tallulah Lyons

It's early morning and I step out onto my screened-in back porch. Three steps forward and I freeze. My heart stops. Right in front of me on the rug is a giant bullfrog – the biggest frog I've ever seen. We lock eyes. It feels like my body is melting into a trance-like fascination and I'm filled with awe. I hear myself speaking softly, "It's ok. It's ok."

Heat radiates into and from my hands as I pick up a dishtowel from a nearby table and reach toward the frog, never losing eye contact. I put the towel around his body and lift him from the floor. I can feel his heart beating. We stare at one another as I slowly carry him across the deck out into the garden. I set him on the ground, bend down, and we continue to gaze at one another for several more seconds. It's a sacred encounter. My heart is filled with love. Then he turns and hops away.

The spell is broken, and I feel sure that some giant underlying fear inside me has been transformed. I feel deep gratitude and a renewed commitment to tend the mystery of dreams and synchronistic events in the waking world.

This and other synchronicities intermingled with Tallulah's frog dreams over more than a decade, during which this next dream stands out as particularly memorable:

Descending to the Camp of the Golden Frogs
Tallulah Lyons

I'm about 16 years old, on a bicycle tour with several other teenagers. We're cycling through a beautiful mountain region when suddenly, just before the road becomes a steep upward incline, we see a road to the right with a big sign and arrow pointing to "Camp of the Golden Frogs." I'm elated when I see the sign and with no hesitation, I swing off to the right. Most of the bikers proceed up the mountain, but one of the boys peels off from the others and joins me. We laugh as the wind blows through our hair and we coast down the long descent to the Camp of the Golden Frogs.

Tallulah's youthful self is on a challenging uphill journey (toward growth, increasing maturity and individuation) when she sees a bold sign that she knows is meant for her. Companioned by her adolescent masculine energy, she makes a turn to the right, toward something coming up into consciousness. Together they coast down a long descent toward the frog wisdom (the golden reality), which she has always had deep within.

This dream provided Tallulah another affirmation of her expanding relationship with the unconscious – particularly with shadow aspects of her life. "Frogs have brought assurance of guiding presence whenever psyche is ready for me to move into the expanding unknown," she said.

As she prepared her dreams for this book, Tallulah welcomed other synchronicities. "One morning when I was out on my porch writing about my frog encounters, two tiny frogs hopped into the birdbath and frolicked around like kids in a swimming pool. It was the first time I have seen frogs this year, and I imagined that Frog, an archetypal symbol for transformation, was happy to be remembered."

A short time later she and her husband moved to a cottage in a retirement village. "The day I arrived I opened my back door and five tiny frogs leaped out of the pine straw by the door. I felt most welcomed."

Pause

*What dream creature is a harbinger of transformation for you?
Which of your attitudes, behaviors or
viewpoints might be ripe for change?*

Ancestral Callings

I will pour out my Spirit on all people.
Your sons and daughters will prophesy,
your old men will dream dreams,
your young men will see visions.

Bible - Joel 2:28

In 1977 I joined millions of other viewers to experience the powerful TV mini-series based on Alex Haley's novel, *Roots*. This fictionalized account of his family's history follows an eighteenth-century forebear from the time he was sold into slavery in Africa, helping to bring into the consciousness of persons of all races a desire to know more about our histories, origins and connections to family and place.

When I moved from Dallas to Houston in the early 90s, I felt uprooted as I visited churches to find a new place to call my faith home. Sitting in the back row of an adult class one Sunday, I chatted with a woman who seemed to feel as out of place as I did. Her flowing hair and flowery muumuu illustrated her story as she told me about leaving Hawaii due to her husband's job transfer and her longing to return home. While I've remained at that church, the other woman disappeared within a few weeks of our conversation and I've often hoped that she has found her way back to the Hawaiian mountains that called so insistently to her spirit.

In earlier chapters, we have seen ways that specific animals, even prehistoric creatures, point us toward old material closeted in the psyche. Here we will look at direct dream references to generational history and inner landscapes as exemplified by two dreamers.

Our first dream is offered by Margie O., who has become an avid genealogist in recent years, tracking her ancestors and preserving the history of her immediate family for her children. In this dream, her mother, who died 35 years earlier, makes an unforgettable appearance:

The Gorilla
Margie O.

A large, black male gorilla is carrying me under his left arm up the left side of a rocky cliff. The group of people I'm with have gone exploring so they're not aware I've been captured. The gorilla takes me around to the back side of the flat-topped cliff to an enclosure in the rock where he can keep me prisoner.

He puts me down inside, barricades the entrance and leaves. It's dark inside and I search for a long time for a way out. I'm about to give up when I find a narrow opening that I can get through that allows me to escape. When I exit the enclosure, I realize I've come out a distance to the right of where the gorilla put me in. I make it back down from the cliff to the ground where he found me.

The others are not back yet. Adrenaline has me alert and aware of my surroundings. I sit and try to catch my breath. As I wait for the others to return, I look up and see the gorilla moving up the cliff with another woman under his arm. I know I must try to help her. I wait for the gorilla to leave and then make my way up the cliff. I get to the entrance and call to the woman. I pull down the barrier so she can come out.

She comes out and her face is unlike any I've seen. It is ghostly white – not a pale white caused by fear but an unnatural luminous white. I stare into her face and am surprised to see that she is my mother.

We can easily understand how this tale, reminiscent of King Kong, earned Big Dream status for Margie. "The big, black male gorilla represents a part of me that was hidden and has not been allowed to express itself. Now it's ignored by all the other parts of me (members of her group) who go off in an entirely different direction, leaving me alone with this shadow part of myself."

Reflecting upon her actions and responses in the dream, Margie finds two distinct ego stances. "In the beginning of the dream, my ego is passive." Fearful in real life of sheer mountain drop-offs, she's strangely ambivalent about dangling from the gorilla's left arm around her waist as he climbs with his right hand. "I'm just observing myself going along with the large, dark shadow taking me prisoner. I (the gorilla) must kidnap myself (the ego) to force myself to look deeply into the conflict that's residing within and holding me prisoner."

Imprisoned at the top of the cliff by this great energy, Margie is forced to remain in darkness and fight through her inner conflict. "It's difficult almost to the point of giving up, but I am finally ready to find freedom and awareness (the light). When I escape the enclosure, I am off to the right, the direction of logic and critical thinking as opposed to the emotional part of myself where the shadow dwelled." From that point, Margie descends the cliff, "going down into the unconscious to reflect on my reluctance to integrate the energy that has limited me and kept me from being my authentic, grounded self."

In the second part of the dream, Margie's ego springs into action, ready to fight for the other woman whom she sees the gorilla carrying up the rocky cliff. "So I go back up to release this other part of me from being kept prisoner." When she removes the barrier for the other woman, this hostage steps into the light. To Margie's great shock, the woman is her mother. "This is an overpowering experience," Margie said. "I see my mother's ghostly luminous white presence. I've been unable since to express in words what she looks like even though it's important."

For several years, this numinous dream resisted processing because of its sheer power. Today Margie embraces it as the divine encounter she knows it to be. Her life-changing moment in her mother's presence reminds her of several Biblical scenes. "When Moses came down from Mt. Sinai with the two stone tablets containing the Ten Commandments, his face was radiant because he had spoken with the Lord." He placed a veil over his face when he was with the Hebrew people but removed the veil only when he went into the tent of meeting where he met the Lord face to face. (Exodus 34:29-35)

Another compelling passage for Margie is the transfiguration of Jesus when he took three of his disciples up a high mountain. "There he was transfigured before them. His face shone like the sun, and his clothes became as white as the light. Just then appeared before them Moses and Elijah, talking with Jesus." (Matthew 17:2-3; see also the gospels of Mark and Luke). Both Moses and Elijah had powerful encounters with God on a mountain (Exodus 33:21-23 and 1 Kings 19:9-11), strengthening the relationship between Old Testament and New Testament events and the juxtaposition of the mountains/rocks and the transfiguration in Margie's dream.

She is placed in a cleft in a rock by her powerful heart energy (gorilla) as a precursor to her mother's coming as a divine messenger at the precise moment she is ready. "This dream reintroduces me to my mother and we make eye contact in an exchange that would not be possible with spoken words." Today her dream continues revealing its wisdom as she ponders its invitation to reevaluate her ideas, feelings and judgments from the past. "I can now see my relationship with Mother as if viewing it from a mountaintop, seeing it from an adult perspective rather than from a child's view."

Meanwhile, Margie's gorilla has taken up residence in her heart, lending its steady nature and qualities of compassionate, protective leadership to her own family. "This archetypal figure is strong enough to carry me through the rocky places to a clifftop where I am held hostage but not harmed, where I become aware of what in me needs to change." Claiming this great inner strength, Margie is going through a process of integration and transformation. "As Gorilla, I have not only rescued myself but also my mother and the deeper truths about our relationship. This dream is helping to free me from what I have barricaded for years within my unconscious."

While Margie's dream provides a faith-filled view of her ties with her late mother, the next dream takes us into an expansive realm of unknown ancestors and the dreamer's sense of place within the world.

We previously met Sarah Norton through her jaguar dream series in *Cats: The Wild Ones*. The following dream occurred when Sarah was in graduate school, working toward her Ph.D., and it went unrecorded for a while due to time constraints, yet remained distinct in her memory. Since then, Sarah has shared it in several dream groups and accomplished some evocative SoulCollage work as part of her ongoing engagement with the dream images. Here is her dream:

Go North!
Sarah D. Norton

I am at a rustic log cabin at the base of a mountain range. It feels like Colorado but perhaps farther north than I have ever been. I'm looking out the back door and see my grandmother out in a garden. I see her jump in surprise at something. Suddenly the scene changes.

I am now right where my grandmother was standing and there's a white snake in front of me. As I watch it slither away, it begins to morph, to change shape. It becomes a white seal, a little less bright white than the snake, with a tinge of orange from the soil under it. Then the seal becomes a large polar bear, also white, but now the orange tinge is brighter, and many shades of the red clay can be seen. As I watch, the orange tint begins to take shape and I can see what looks almost like cave paintings on the bear's fur. The shapes show the animals as they transformed from one into another, the snake, the seal, the bear and now also the face of a man. As the bear continues away up the base of the mountain, I see its silhouette beginning to change. By the time the bear reaches the tree line, it is a man. The man continues walking into the woods. I know he is headed to the far north and I feel an urge to follow.

The title that this dream selected for itself reminds Sarah of her step-grandfather saying, "Go north, young man," and encouraging her with his adventurous spirit. "I grew up in north Georgia and often traveled to North Carolina as a child," she said. "So *north* invokes a feeling of home for these reasons, and there's something about the idea of north that is comfortable and cozy to me."

Sarah recognizes other deep roots in the dream. "In waking life, my maternal grandfather had a cabin in Colorado, so the dream setting feels like a place of the ancestors in many ways. The history of my father's line begins in a town called Nord-Hagen (literally *from a northern village*) in Norway." This place-name/surname, Nordhagen, became Norton when the family immigrated to the U.S., and for Sarah, this heritage has always provided inspiration, a strong affinity for Norse mythology, and a resonant sense of *north*.

On a personal spiritual level, Sarah spent many years as part of a drum circle where the direction north in the medicine wheel is the place of ancestors and wisdom. "In my mind, as a student of depth psychology and Jung, this is also the place of the unconscious. So going north has many connotations, from personal to collective levels of meaning and importance."

The creatures in this dream are unexpected. Though Sarah has previously dreamed of snakes, the seal and bear are new to her dreamscape. "Each of the animals holds its own archetypal energy," she said, adding that the seal reminds her of the Celtic myth in which a seal sheds its skin to walk on land as a human woman. "When combined into one creature, the creatures speak to me of wholeness. The snake slithers on and beneath the ground, the seal swims in the water, and the bear runs upon the land. So everywhere on and in the earth can be reached by these three creatures. The man who arises from these beastly forms is like an ancestral figure – almost a shaman – and there is magic to learn from the northern mountains and the forest there. I want to follow him to learn more about where he was going and his ancient ways."

When she awakened from this dream, she initially felt the absence of a bird in flight, which would have completed a quaternity of creatures. But the more she experiences her narrative, the more she realizes that the aspect of flight is present, dwelling in the man with his intellect. In Sarah's dream world, flying is a common symbol for the heights to which the human intellect can carry us. "However," she said, "the high-flying mind of man suffers when it's not grounded by physical experience. That's why it is comforting to me that the man arises from these very grounded animals." She also relates this tension to her waking life challenge of balancing the academic language of her dissertation with a grounding in personal stories.

The polar bear holds a special place in the dream, in the process of change, and in current climate issues. "The bear represents an evolution not only in how it morphs from these literally, spatially lower animals into the man walking upright, but also in the colors of its coat. The cultural evolution of the mind is expressed in the cave paintings." The astonishing drawings on the bear's white fur also remind Sarah of her roots in the red clay of north Georgia and of the colors of alchemical transformation. "The orange of the red earth on the animal's white coat is the rubedo (red) rising from the alchemical albedo (white), the rising of something new, the promise of a new day."

Not surprisingly Sarah connects her dream bear to climate issues as well. While she feels the image of the polar bear on a shrinking iceberg has lost much of its impact through overuse in recent years, the plight of the polar bear nevertheless speaks to her heart. "At the time of the dream, I was working deeply with the idea of north in the melting of the polar ice caps as a result of the climate crisis. [Her dissertation title is *Arctic Imaginings: Chasing Ice through C.G. Jung's Liber Novus into the 21st Century*.] I was continuously reading about places to the north geographically and high in elevation – places where so much of our climatological memory in the form of ice core data is being lost as the ice melts." Relating to the theme of grounding, she added the caution that focusing solely on scientific data about climate issues can, in fact, obscure the grounded reality of the negative and lasting effects many people are feeling.

In conclusion, Sarah has received *Go North!* as a deeply archetypal and inspirational dream. "The connection of the human and animal, the ancestral nature of the place, and the man who walks into the wood are very comforting for me. It was medicine for my dissertation journey and is still unfolding for me today. It is one of those dreams that I will revisit year after year and still find new meaning."

Pause

Who among your ancestors is whispering
to you through your dreams?
What is your sense of earth's places and creatures
as part of your own human story?

Community Connections

Cognitive ethology is the comparative, evolutionary, and ecological study of animal minds. It focuses on how animals think and what they feel, and this includes their emotions, beliefs, reasoning, information processing, consciousness, and self-awareness.... Flexibility in behavior is one of the litmus tests for consciousness, for a mind at work.

Marc Bekoff

The principle that dreams are given for our healing and wholeness creates a nourishing and supportive perspective for the journeys of countless dreamers. In preceding chapters, we've walked with dreamers as they've confronted a broad spectrum of issues and insights that have benefitted them in deeply personal ways. None of us, however, exists in a vacuum. We're alternately prodded, bombarded, inspired and appalled by events and circumstances in the environments where we exist, in the collective, the outer world.

The following dreams direct our attention to this outward dimension, as dreamers share thought-provoking encounters with religious, racial, cultural and political issues – giving us new perspectives on living in our challenged and challenging world.

For example:

Two Dogs Killed by a Car

I'm in the yard with my husband when there's a commotion up the road to the right. Pete tells me that a neighbor's dogs which have been running around without leashes have been run over. This isn't far from our house. I see two large dogs lying on the side of the road and two other dogs frantically trying to rouse them – nosing and prodding, whining and howling in an almost human way of expressing grief.

At the time of this dream, I'd just learned of two friends who were grieving the deaths of their pet dogs, but I knew that more was going on here than the obvious connection to that waking life trigger. Since restraint and control are common themes for me, it follows that I'm disturbed when free-ranging animals are injured. Even more pertinent, my daytime emotions were *running wild* at the time due to turmoil and change within my church. Opposing views (the two pairs of dogs) captured the essence of the conflict. The struggle was so intense that some disgruntled church members (perceiving themselves run over by events) simply went away (died to us), leaving the rest of us mourning the loss for our community (the dogs howling with human-like sounds).

As the previous dream illustrates, faith community discord can generate strong and painful feelings – perhaps because such clashes deliver a mortal blow to the idealistic belief (or hope) that religious folk should be able to rise above the more negative aspects of human nature.

Consider this dream account shared by a man who was serving a stressful term as his church council chair:

Bear Hunt
Anonymous

I am hunting bear with dogs. I have just completed one difficult chase and am going back to the exact spot that I'd started that chase from in order to begin again. As I near that spot I see four light brown/tan bears crossing a pasture. They seem to be on a road in the pasture, an inverted L-shape seen from my location. The bears are around the bend, lumbering along.

I back my truck up to the fence and let the dogs out of the box sending them down the road. One of the four dogs is long-haired with a long, feathered tail. My impression is it is a golden retriever or a setter. *The dogs strike the trail and soon are chasing the bears by sight. They slow as they catch up to the bears and are not as excited as they should be.*

Suddenly I am concerned that they are after someone's cows. In my dream, the bears have changed into cows!

♥

On the previous night, the dreamer had attended a meeting regarding a critical report on the health of his church. This dream struck him as such sharply relevant commentary on that situation that he subsequently shared it with the pastor and the consultant who'd been brought in to help resolve the painful internal conflict.

The dreamer recognizes the four bears as the four pastors who had led the church since its founding two decades earlier. "The first three pastors had been chased away by our congregation," he said, "and the fourth was currently under pressure (going around the bend). Elements of the congregation have seen each of our pastors as dangerous or threatening to the wellbeing of the church." He sees this dream revealing how the church kept starting over in the same place with every new pastor (return to the exact spot where the last chase had begun). "The fence represents the barriers between the congregation (including me) and the pastors." As an experienced hunter, this dreamer is surprised at the golden retriever among the hounds until, during his processing, he remembers that one of the most vocal critics among the church members owned a golden retriever.

He watches the pack of dogs (the people hounding the pastors) take off after the bears. But strangely the dogs lose their excitement for the hunt as they near their quarry. When they see the morphed creatures (better understanding the real situation), they find less to bark about. To the dreamer, the cows represent the pastors as they truly were – not intentionally dangerous or threatening but nurturing, a willing source of spiritual nourishment. As the leader of the congregation (keeper of the dogs), the dreamer knows at the end that he must catch the dogs and put them back in their box on the truck. "This accurately reflects and reinforces my opinion that I need to work to calm the situation at church," he said.

While instinctual animal energy is powerfully evident in this dream, the *four* dogs and *four* bears also point to strength and stability, an orderly, foundational quality. Similarly they "square up" with the four aspects of human nature – sensation, feeling, thought and intuition – all of which encouraged this dreamer to work with renewed energy toward the harmony his church so desperately needed.

We have already journeyed through a series of Emma Adeline's dreams in the *Snakes* chapter, but the following snake dream stands apart both in its content and import. Coming at a time when she and her husband lived in temporary lodging as their home was razed and rebuilt following a hurricane-related flood, the dream's message reaches beyond her personal insights to offer observations on her place within her communities and the world:

Two Sides of the Same Coin
Emma Adeline R.

I am sitting and visiting with two or three people when I see (maybe on TV or in person) a man draped over a tree limb. He is very still as if dead. I notice what appears to be his arm moving, then I realize it's a very large snake moving across his body. And I can see that the snake is the full length of his body. As the snake moves, I see that the man's leg has a wound on it as if the snake has bitten him. The flesh is broken; there's not much blood but it needs to be cleaned and bandaged.

Then my "camera" view pulls back so that I can see the whole scene and the snake has moved off the man's body. I am talking to the man like a reporter from a distance or via phone: "Did you know there was a snake crawling on you? Did you know your leg was wounded? What are you feeling? Go and get some medical attention."

❦

For Emma Adeline, this came as a powerful message from the Dream Maker, confirming her long-standing commitment to social justice and to "the personal and societal exhaustion resulting from the wounds of masculine domination."

She sees the opening close-up view as representing individuals and the next scene (the shift in "camera" view) as representing the larger systemic challenges of society. "What I observe in this dream is that men suffer from masculine domination as much as women. The injury on the man's leg speaks to the nature of the wound – damage to the grounding of one's identity and to the foundation of societal values." She points to the Biblical reference (Numbers 21:6-9) that explains that healing comes from identifying and being willing to look directly at injury. "It is cooperation between the conscious and unconscious that brings health and wholeness," she said. Similarly, she sees the wound and the healing as two sides of the same coin. "The gentle, protective snake reminds us that our humanity and connection with Spirit will hold and guide us as we move toward individuation and service to others."

All of this raises a long-standing question for Emma Adeline. Which is more important: the individual or the community? "The dream's two scenes and multiple interpretations remind me that an individual is only as healthy as the community and vice versa, thus changing a duality question into unity." Her research into numbers – the twoness that the Greeks called the Dyad – led Emma Adeline to observe all the qualities of two: opposites, conflict, peacemakers, partnership, and unity. She also sees a proliferation of opposites – details/big picture; individual/society; wounding/healing; masculine/feminine; conscious/unconscious – recognizing that this is often an indicator of coming change.

In reflecting on this dream and the problems prevalent in the surrounding environment at that time and the persistent racial challenges of the present, Emma Adeline said, "Society needs to value and engage with conflict and healthy critique, yet hold it in balance so that it does not become oppression."

Tallulah Lyons, who shared her frog dreams for the *Transformation* chapter, tells of a forceful Big Dream that she had on three separate occasions: *"I see a woman stuck in a box that is wedged in the middle of a steep staircase. I know that she must scream to get help if she is to become unstuck."* After much work with her stuck-in-a-box dream, Tallulah had this awareness: "I decided that psyche was calling me to find my voice and to speak out about the current political and social crises that swamp our world. This felt like a daunting challenge because all my life, I have focused on individual transformation."

Into this context she had the following dream:

The Miniature Whale
Tallulah Lyons

I feel something stirring in the back of my throat and I somehow know that it is a totally transparent, miniature whale. In the middle of the whale's stomach is a globe of the earth. I also realize that at the back of the throat of every person in the world is a miniature whale, each with a globe inside.

In the dream, I feel I have just realized something extremely important, but I'm unsure what it is. I want to understand and tell everyone. I feel excited, yet unsure of what to do next. When I wake up, I draw a sketch of the little whale in my journal.

Tallulah immediately spotted the connection with her stuck-in-a-box dream. For her, the miniature whale dream emerged as "an amazing symbol created by the wisdom of the unconscious. It seems to be an image of assurance and affirmation that everyone in the whole world has within them the capacity to speak truth. The image is a gift that allows me a quick encounter with a giant force concentrated within us all that helps us give voice to the reality that we are one people. I feel immense gratitude and renewed courage to keep trying to expand my voice."

Although the whale doesn't appear in physical form, Tallulah knows the reality of its presence. We can see in her dream a clear (transparent) message for community as well as for her personally – a call to all thinking people of the world to access their power, find their voices and band together as a great force of deep truth.

While Tallulah's dream focuses on the need for *voice*, my dream that follows emphasizes the need for *sight*. During 2020 my intense frustration over the tattered political climate in the United States and the global pandemic led to this distressing imagery:

Horse with No Eyes

I'm watching a man walking along with an open horse-drawn cart. It feels like a medieval scene. The man speaks harshly to the horse: "Don't you be looking around now!"

As I look at the horse, I see that he has two oversized empty eye sockets. How could he look around at anything! I'm shocked. The man stoops down to pick up a wrapped body from the ground and places it on the cart with another wrapped body.

Although COVID-19 was just beginning its sweep across the U.S., this scene is reminiscent of the Black Death with carts circulating through the streets and cries ringing out: "Bring out your dead!" This is unmistakably a dream about the collective as well as my waking life sorrow and anxiety about the political landscape. *What on earth can I do about the things that trigger my furious reactions to the evening news?* It seems clear that the politicians whose behavior I find abhorrent are counting on me (and the rest of the population) to ignore or overlook *("Don't you be looking around now!")* the real truths behind their words and actions and the consequences that follow.

This sightless horse is my own power, stifled, harnessed and blinded. How can I escape the oppressive bindings to live more fully? What parts of our culture (individuals, groups, values, principles, institutions) are suffering, dying and carted away? The huge empty eye sockets of this creature remind me of all the New Testament references to sight.

Lord, give me eyes to see! Help me reclaim my own power!

Now we turn to the dream series of Kris, an African-American woman with Cherokee and Creek Native American roots. Kris grew up worshipping in the African Methodist Episcopal Church in Tulsa, Oklahoma, where social justice was woven into the theological fabric of the church and community and she learned to embrace it as a reflection of righteousness and a worthy pursuit for all people of faith. Looking back, she said, "Although I did not think of it like this at the time, I embody social justice. Throughout my life and career, I've walked in places and sat in spaces where few people who look like me have … or could." Before entering vocational ministry and marriage, Kris provided spiritual support to women, children, veterans, and others whom Jesus might call "the least of these."

Kris's dream creature, the tiger, burst into consciousness in the summer of 2020, a few months into the COVID-19 pandemic and preceding the hotly contested presidential election. "The timing corresponded with the horrific death of George Floyd, which reflected the worst type of inhumane treatment leading to the premature death of far too many Black people in police custody," she said. "Consequently, protests erupted all over the United States and all around the world supporting Mr. Floyd, his family and the Black Lives Matter Movement."

This places Kris's dream series squarely in the context of systemic inequalities and injustices against those perceived as "the other," not only within the U.S. but in many places around the world. Through the trio of dreams that follow, she received guidance and wrestled with new awareness about her role in this painfully divisive time.

The beginning:

Let the Tiger Out
Kris

I am in the kitchen in a house that isn't mine. There on a bed in an adjacent room a tiger lies peacefully. The tiger comes into the kitchen and begins to drink from an industrial-sized, gray pot of potato soup. I realize the tiger might not be satisfied and may want more than just soup, so I decide to let the tiger out as a precaution. I walk the tiger to the front door, and she follows like an excited puppy, ready to go outside.

The house has a wrap-around porch and three doors in one: a screen door, a glass storm door and an interior door. The framing of the screen door is fragile and barely holding onto the rest of the door frame. I ask my husband about the screen door and he helps me close it.

We all move into the living area where eight or more people from all backgrounds are present – men, women, black, white, latinx, young, old, etc. My husband welcomes two black men, maybe his cousins, into the house. When they enter the room, I invite them to sit on the couch or wherever they are most comfortable. Shakira is there, giving a promotional demonstration involving exercise equipment – *a trapeze-like rowing machine. As Shakira completes her demonstration, I notice that this is a welcoming environment where everyone can be themselves. Here they are seen, heard and respected as fellow-contributors to a worthy cause and society as a whole.*

The dream opens with Kris in a house that doesn't seem like her own (an unfamiliar part of psyche) where she encounters her tiger energy at rest. Its drinking from the big pot of potato soup has strong communal associations for the dreamer. The pot is large enough to feed many people, reminding her of the *Feed my Sheep* ministry she'd once launched at her local church. She recalls potato soup as a dish that can be stretched to nourish many. "However, the tiger's drinking was almost gratuitous as if to say, 'I am one with you and this community.'"

A critical aspect of this dream is Kris's response to the possibility that the tiger might still be hungry – which might be perceived as a dangerous threat to the others in her home. "I felt that I should take her out of the house as protection for the human guests and for herself," said Kris, adding, *"I'm concerned that others may fear the tiger in the same way that many people project their fears onto black men."*

The wrap-around front porch has a friendly, welcoming feeling. However, the triple front door, with its trinitarian connotation, seems delicately constructed. Kris sees the screen door as fragile, and the door frame as a decision point, a threshold that goes both ways. Notably, it is her pastor husband who shows her how the screen works, suggesting that her rational masculine energy might take the lead in discerning (screening out or in) the truths that need to be revealed.

The presence of world-famous entertainer Shakira adds an intriguing element. Born to a Lebanese father and Columbian mother, Shakira honors both her Arabic and Latin heritages in her music. As a dancer, she displays an energetic athleticism that is here converted into her displaying a way to embrace and *exercise* diversity and acceptance. "People are often unified by entertainers and sports figures," Kris commented, "and Shakira's demonstration seems to say let's get to work, let's get moving, on a social, political, and physical level."

Kris knows that the diverse group of people in the living room have congregated for a reason. "The goal is healing," she said. "The people are coming together with a oneness of purpose – to collaborate by having conversations that society would say are uncomfortable. Yet the people in the dream are comfortable in this space, able to be themselves. They can all be seen, heard and respected as fellow contributors to a worthy cause and society." And Kris understands, at least in part, her own responsibility within this endeavor.

This dream, she said, laid a foundation for what was to come – a call to action that develops further in her next two dreams. The same night that Kris had shared *Let the Tiger Out* with her dream group, her tiger returned, more insistent than before:

Tiger's Back Home
Kris

I am in my house and I notice Tiger lying comfortably on the floor next to the couch as I go into the kitchen. Tiger follows and jumps onto the kitchen counter. I can tell she has lost a little weight since the last time I saw her. I start to make my way toward the front door. She roars as if to communicate something directly to me.

I calmly call three times to my sister who is in another room as I don't want to acknowledge my fear — whatever it might be. Then, knowing I am dreaming, I make a decision to go back and embrace Tiger to see what she is trying to say to me. I apologize for almost sending her away a second time.

Tiger (who now has a capital-letter name) refuses to be ignored! Kris and her powerful energy meet once again in the kitchen, which she calls a place of necessity and nourishment. This encounter is literally *on the counter*, putting Tiger in a position where Kris must look up at her. Yet Tiger has not been well-tended or nourished (she's lost weight) since their last encounter. And she roars "like the Lion of Judah as if to say, *Listen, I'm here and this is the way.*" We might also wonder if Tiger is saying that Kris's processing with her dream group was just the beginning, that there's far more nourishing wisdom to be shared.

Kris's apprehension is understandable. Tiger now presents a more confrontational energy than did the more placid, puppy-like tiger of her first dream. Kris calls out to her protective, nurturing older sister, whom she describes as "an angel on a mission and a powerful pray-er." She calls three times, a reference again to the trinity, before she realizes that she must face Tiger alone. Upon reflection, Kris acknowledged that her off-stage dream sister surely would have heard the commotion and responded if this were something to be handled by someone else. But this is Kris's psychic decision point. In a lucid moment, she realizes, "This isn't ominous. This is opportunity." And she turns to engage her Tiger.

Excited by this reappearance of her personal Tiger, Kris's processing centered on the Magic Questions. Tiger answered the questions in this way: "I am Tiger. My purpose is to abide and sound the alarm. I like being Tiger because I am strong. I don't like being alone, isolated or feared. I fear being misunderstood and rejected due to my presumed predatory nature. I want to live. I want to eat well. I want companionship. If I could talk, I would tell you, Fear not." To Kris, this was a comforting message and she connected Tiger's words biblically: "When angels show up in the scriptures, they often say, 'Fear not.'"

This dream further magnifies the message of her first dream, using Tiger to highlight the unnecessary fears relating to a *presumed predatory nature*. "I see my dream Tiger as the embodiment of all of our racial and interpersonal fears," Kris said. "Tiger is not showing up to maim or devour but to help heal race relations through presence, dialogue, and understanding."

Two months after her second visit from Tiger, Kris had a third dream that signified further deepening in consciousness:

Your Tiger, Not Mine
Kris

I am moving from one living space to another, two floors up. Then I am walking west on a sidewalk outside a familiar church. On the northwest corner stand two men talking. One man wears a black fez and holds a rope connected to a tiger. The second man has neatly cut, shiny black hair but no hat. The tiger doesn't have stripes but is a brownish-yellowish-orangish color with fuzzy fur. As the two men talk, the tiger slips off its leash and starts walking east toward me. I think this tiger looks more like a big cat – I don't like cats – but I want to test its temperament, so I lie down. The tiger doesn't charge at me or avoid me. He simply continues advancing slowly in my direction, almost with curiosity and concern.

I stand up and start walking towards the men on the corner to let them know their tiger is off its leash. The tiger follows me as I call out to them. At first, the man without a hat is a bit stand-offish. When I ask him where he got his tiger, he said, "Iran." I'm not sure if he is serious or being sarcastic. I respond by telling him that I have been studying the types of tigers in the region, spanning from India to Russia. His demeanor changes to a more welcoming disposition and he smiles. I then address the man with the black fez. Knowing this tiger is not mine, I'm curious about where these men and this tiger have come from.

This dream opens with a transition and upward movement in the psyche. The two floors up may signify an impending union within the spiritual realm – mirrored by the grounding in faith which we see in the presence of a familiar church. Then comes the introduction of the foreign element on a corner (an intersection of directions, cultures, ways of life), which reminds us of the diversity of persons in Kris's living room in the first dream. "In this dream, maybe I've arrived at where I've been going," she said, alluding to the invitation and the challenge it presents to her.

For Kris, the black fez points to "doing good," even though the color is different from the signature red fez of the Shriners who operate the Shriners Hospitals for Children[R]. Also, the black fez and the black hair of the other man suggest that both men are from the east. Yet Kris is walking westward, indicating a union or communion with their differences. Notice the connection between these men and Shakira's appearance (her Lebanese-Arab heritage) in Kris's first tiger dream.

Even the tiger itself is from abroad (Iran). Although similar in stature to the first two dream tigers, this one is slimmer and more like a lioness. The previous animals display the traditional striped (defined) tiger pattern of orange and black, but this tiger wears a melding of less-defined, more unified colors and a textured (fuzzy) coat. Working with Robert Hoss's Color Questionnaire regarding her first two tigers, Kris found several resonances with orange as signifying openness and an expansion of interests and influence. This tiger, with coloring that one might expect on a domesticated Asiatic lioness introduces a new element. We sense here a further taming of this mighty big cat energy that might enable her to integrate it and bring it forth more effectively into her waking life.

Interestingly, her dream ego's act of lying down before this tiger (to test its intention) is a familiar posture of surrender in the animal world. Fortunately, this tiger is gentle (even curious and concerned) and wants attention. We also see that this tiger who is *not mine* is definitely hers in that it comes to meet her, claim her and, not only follows her back to the men at the intersection but serves as the catalyst to open communication beyond the familiar. Notice that the conversation with the hatless man, though it begins awkwardly (is he serious or sarcastic?), becomes more congenial when she explains that she is studying tigers (integrating her dream creature's energy and essence), which gains his approval.

Considering the arc of her tiger dream series, Kris said that her first dream laid the foundation for her call to action, which was clarified in the second dream and further defined in this third dream. Here she is drawn away from the familiar and into new territory for which her first and second dreams have prepared her.

"In what ways have the isms of our society shaped how I view others?" she asked. "And how open can I be if I'm ignorant of other cultures? This dream seems an in-my-face challenge to confront some of my own areas of bias, and to study and get to know people beyond my familiar circles."

As a black woman who knows what it is like to be discounted, feared or even hated, Kris has embraced her tiger both as messenger and companion who can help her open herself at a deeper level concerning all of the "others" in the world. "It is only through seeing our reactions to others that we can learn and see who we really are," she said. "Only then can we know ourselves and our true character."

This chapter might be seen as dreamwork at its most far-reaching. All of our inner work, our treasured insights and awakenings, are marvelous for us individually, and there's much to gain from all of that. Yet if we follow a faith or philosophy that calls us to be present to others, to see a bigger picture and live for a higher purpose beyond ourselves, we should watch our dreams for their wider significance, then ask ourselves how we might respond.

Pause

*What dream creature is nudging me toward
greater compassion for others?
How is the Dream Maker calling me to be
present in our troubled world?*

The Promise of More to Come

Every child should have mud pies, grasshoppers, water bugs, tadpoles, frogs, mud turtles .... woodchucks, bats, bees, butterflies, various animals to pet ... and any child who has been deprived of these has been deprived of the best part of education.

Luther Burbank

My love for animals extends its roots back to my family's modeling and to Seattle's Woodland Park Zoo. Wondering how dramatically the zoo may have changed in the decades since my childhood visits, I realized I could go there right then, from the computer on my desk. So I did. Immediately a little creature dubbed #SEATTLEWATERMELON, captured my heart. This portly little Malayan tapir, named Sempurna by the time I viewed her online, sports a distinctive spotted and watermelon-striped camouflage infant-tapir onesie and lives with her mama in the zoo's lush Tropical Asia habitat. There, if I were to visit in person, I could commune with them as well as with the Malayan tiger, sloth bear, orangutan and warty pig. Today's modern Woodland Park Zoo is a stunning transformation from the mid-twentieth century zoo where I marveled with crowds at exotic creatures who paced and stared back at us from their stark and stony enclosures. That was the way all zoos were, pre-enlightenment.

So, what did I learn from my virtual zoo visit? I found myself questioning whether or not my intentional soul work of dream-tending has informed and modernized the environment of my heart. Do I ever stuff my dream creatures into bare enclosures in my psyche designed primarily for my protection? Or do I attempt to welcome them into natural habitats that I create within?

The current treasure on my coffee table is *The Photo Ark*, a National Geographic book comprised of 400 stunning animal portraits by the dedicated and gifted photographer Joel Sartore[1]. Each creature, respectfully captured in color against a plain black or white backdrop, invites the viewer into its reality. Here I marvel at a giant anteater with her pup riding on her back; a meditative Celebes crested macaque; a platypus displaying its duck-like bill and webbed feet; an incredible facial closeup of a Mexican hairy dwarf porcupine; a red, stick-like Atlantic sea spider, an aptly named (and truly remarkable to me!) giant snake-necked turtle. From facing pages, I am confronted by an Asiatic lion and a Sulawesi stripe-faced fruit bat, both of whom gaze at me, simply and directly, from deep brown eyes.

What do you have to tell me, to show me, about your nature and your name?

Just as the fluid dynamics of dreamwork hinder most attempts to "put a dream to bed" with nice, concluding remarks, so does this book resist a conclusion. For both writer and reader, dreamwork continually opens new vistas.

Reviewing the well-scribbled pages of my dream journals, I've gained a valuable perspective on my journey from once-upon-a-time to here-and-now. The rivers flowing through my dreamscape have carved new channels of energy and awareness that indicate I've made some progress after all. Like Woodland Park Zoo, I've evolved to higher levels, to greater freedom for my dream animals and more meaningful, enriching interactions between us. Occasionally, as in *MoleCat's Revelation*, I've revisited a years-old dream to discover the riches available only through the probing of a more experienced, compassionate dreamer. I've learned never to assume that I've gathered all that a single dream or a series has to tell me or to imagine that there's not far more for me to learn from dreams yet to come.

Naturally, as I compiled dreams for this book the Dream Maker didn't take a vacation. Compelling animal appearances continued:

Return of the White Cat

I'm in my living room when I see that a young, slender white cat has come in. To my surprise, she walks among our five gray and

Dream Animal Wisdom

black cats and they all behave calmly with no territorial howling or hissing. That's really surprising!

I'm glad to see this cat wears a collar so I don't need to worry about her. I pick her up and carry her out into the neighborhood to find where she's from. A woman across the street tells me the neighbor beyond her is the one who owns the cat.

When I get to that house, I'm met by a pleasant dark-haired woman who acknowledges that the cat is hers. But she seems ambivalent about accepting the white cat as if she is waiting for me to comprehend something that she feels I should already know. I feel a little odd about it.

I received this dream 15 years after *The White Cat and the Insect Queen* (*Cats* chapter) and many months after my experience described in *MoleCat's Revelation*. Ironically, in this dream, my territorial real-life housecats don't fuss about our spiritual visitor. This should tell me that the white cat already belongs, but I'm not quite ready to comprehend that. My response to seeing her collar mirrors how I would react in waking life, with relief that she is not another homeless cat needing care. But returning this cat to her owner doesn't go as expected. That aspect of my personality wonders when I will *finally* get it – understanding that my instinctual energies, including this reemergent one, are all my own. For now, she will tend my white cat for me until I'm ready to claim her and access her special wisdom.

In this second dream, as the 2020 pandemic raged in the outside world, I found an astonishing inner resource of strength:

Safe Within the Storm

I'm in a huge hotel with my high-school friend Joy, when I take off on my own for what becomes an epic journey to find a coffee shop. Along the way, from a top floor window, I see a massive storm with a black funnel cloud coming right at the building. There's a lot of noise and commotion as I crouch on the floor while the storm rolls over.

When I finally locate the coffee shop, more complications arise, and I am still empty-handed when I find myself at a lofty hallway juncture between two big hotels. I can't remember which one I had been in before or exactly where I had left my friend Joy.

Apparently I make a good choice because I suddenly find myself in an inviting, wood-paneled anteroom with a boxy little elevator straight ahead. I think it looks too short for a person, more like it's suited for animals. Next to it, a woman reclines on a sofa.

I turn to the left and enter an amazing room with cats of every size and species – domestic cats on my left and a variety of big cats to my right. Every one of the cats is sleek, beautiful and healthy and they're all sleeping or lounging on chairs and sofas on both sides of the room simply looking at me. All wear red collars. I walk among the cats to an adjacent room where I see a similar scene with dogs – all different sizes and breeds. Every dog is sleek, healthy and beautiful, peacefully at rest. All wear collars.

I would love to linger among all these creatures, but I know that they will remain here and right now I feel I need to move on to find Joy.

♥

This dream was extraordinary. While the storm batters the outer world, I'm safe in a massive structure. I've engaged my inner joy and, though I wander off in search of caffeine, I find instead a far greater source of innate energy. Here are my domestic cat companions as well as wild cats of every species. Yet I must move through and beyond this familiar feline energy to find the warm, relational energy of the dog. The sheer number and variety of animals amaze me, and I understand that I can return here at any time I wish or will, that all this creature power lies within, quietly resting, energy in reserve, all collared, all mine.

A third dream continued the theme of integration:

Giving and Receiving Love

I'm at a rural home where I'm learning how to feed all the cats and dogs who live there and where to find their big bags of food. Outdoors I interact with a cat who's sitting upon a wooden box or shelf near my heart level. It seems a composite of many of my known cats. We are having a wonderful interchange, looking into each other's eyes as I run my hands from its shoulders down the sides of its body.
  I say, "I love you," as I often do to all my known cats.
  To my amazement and joy, this cat looks at me with an almost human-like expression and says: "I love you."

Among my favorite SoulCollage cards is one containing a background image of the starry cosmos. In the foreground, a small child's hand reaches out to touch the paw of a big cat. Beside them gleams a vibrant red heart. I often gaze at this collage as I write.
  My fourth and final dream offering, completing a quaternity, was a recent surprise. While cat and turtle have been my close companions for many years, just like *The Photo Ark* has enlarged my thinking about animals, this dream revealed an expanded psychic awareness:

Joy and Three Horses

I am with my husband and we are in a long war with the British. Pete is captured by the army. Then a squadron of small white helicopters flies in from the right. My friend Joy is flying one of them and I escape with her. She is flying very low.

Then, looking up from the ground, I see three horses dangling from straps beneath the helicopter. Two horses are alike in appearance, but one is smaller, shaggier, wilder looking and I'm concerned about the thin straps holding that horse.

This dream arrived on the eve of the 2020 U.S. presidential election, reminding me that despite my dismay about the political turmoil, joy can lift me above the fray. Simultaneously, I'm reminded of our 1776 war for independence from the British and how the dream suggests that I might claim a new freedom from the proper, buttoned-up behavior I associate with the British. I also recognize a feminine struggle against perceived domination by masculine energy in politics, unfairly projected upon my husband, who is captured and removed from the scene as feminine energy comes to the fore.

The little white helicopters swoop in from my unconscious with a buzzing, *Star-Wars*-like sound effect – an angelic host of rescuers come to save the day. But I'm not merely passive. I must accept Joy's offer of a ride, rather than remain stuck in a negative situation. A low level of flight may be the best way to achieve a healthy balance between solid grounding and lofty spirituality.

My dual perspective (both inside the helicopter and viewing it from the ground) allows me to see the trinity of horses hanging by straps. Two are well-secured with stout straps, but the third one, dangling from much thinner bands, appears smaller, sturdier, stronger and untamed. Although I depend upon the divine for my ultimate rescue, I too play an essential part in my life. Along with my predictable, domesticated energies, I have something wild and wonderful within – more loosely held, but also mine.

I see in this dream the promise of excitement, great hope and maybe some risk. If I can release my emphasis on emotional security, I can fly, and I have some amazing horsepower to carry me on my way.

❣

My friend Robin, an aptly-named avian veterinarian, recently told our Sunday morning group about her anxious moments looking down from a raised wooden walkway in a Texas park as a baby alligator struggled to escape its entanglement in fishing line on the shore below. Suddenly the mother alligator burst from the water, croaking and hissing, and deftly used her fearsome teeth to free her baby from its ensnarement and carry it back to the water.

Those of us present for this telling marveled.

Thinking of this as I pause on my journey, I realize how much more there is to learn about nature and nurturing, about love and compassion and the many forms of connection between creatures. My mind swirls with old and new memories:

Me ... at five years old, living in North Seattle next door to a residual farm where the owner allowed the neighborhood children to play. There I breathed the fertile, earthy smell of cow dung as I sought the delicate three-petalled trilliums in their hiding places beneath the trees. There I came upon a haunting discovery one day in the pasture – a cow's afterbirth, still fresh and glistening, whispering to me the mysterious secrets of new life.

My mother ... a few years later in Eugene, Oregon, keeping vigil through a long night, trying to save a tiny creature who'd been delivered to our back porch by one of our cats. This helpless, hairless, two-inch infant, eyes still closed, had transparent skin that allowed me to see its tender inner parts just as surely as I saw my mother's heart through her gentle care.

Vivie ... a sweet feral cat from one of my colonies, ill, calmly accepting my family's feeding and tending in our garage, safe in a warm kennel with soft towels, soothed by cat music on the CD player. When I finally accepted that her medication was not working, I left my work on this manuscript to sit beside her kennel and read her to sleep the evening before I took her to the vet for release from the suffering her cancer would have caused.

Living forward, I hope to find the courage to plunge into all the new mysteries of sorrow and joy presented to me and to remain there long enough to absorb their lessons. Lately I've pondered the strange little pufferfish, who creates decorative symmetrical circles in the sand on the seafloor.[2] I imagine one of those perfect circles as my own mandala of Self, which I might encounter with a dive deep into my unconscious. There lie the truths the holy Dream Maker has for me.

Dream animal wisdom has been steadily leading me nearer the core of what is wild and wonderful, wise and true. May you come to welcome and honor all of your real and imaginary creatures ... as I do mine.

I see you.
I feel you.
I hear your heartbeat and I know you hear mine.
We are kin.
Let us journey on together.

NOTES

Introduction
A Journey at the Heart Level

Epigraph: Sy Montgomery, *How to be a Good Creature: A Memoir in Thirteen Animals*. Houghton Mifflin Harcourt Publishing Company, 2018. Quote is from the Introduction. I recommend this heartwarming book for any animal lover.

1. Trap-Neuter-Return (TNR), a respected humane program for capping the reproduction of community (feral and stray) cats, is widely used throughout the U.S. and many other developed and developing countries. For more information: alleycatallies.org.

2. Sy Montgomery, *How to be a Good Creature,* p. 198.

3. For an excellent discussion of the history of animal behavior science, see *Beyond Words: What Animals Think and Feel* by Carl Safina, particularly the chapter *Distinctly Human*. Henry Holt and Company, LLC.

4. See National Geographic, June 2019, *The Hidden Cost of Wildlife Tourism*, for a revealing special report about how people who love animals can unknowingly fuel their suffering.

Part I: Creatures in the Spotlight

Epigraph: Robert J. Hoss, MS, *Dream Language: Handbook for Dreamwork,* 2nd Edition, PDF Version 2019, downloaded from dreamscience.org, p. 131, edited.

1. Robert L. Van de Castle, Ph.D., *Our Dreaming Mind: A Sweeping Exploration of the Role That Dreams Have Played in Politics, Art, Religion and Psychology, From Ancient Civilizations to the Present Day.* See Chapter 11, *What's in a Dream?* for his discussion of dream animals.

Dogs: Leashes and Loyalty

Epigraph: from Britannica. The complex story of the human-canine bond goes back for millennia. While dogs are loved and greatly valued in Western civilization, they're not held in high esteem in parts of Asia and developing countries.

[1] *Animal Wise: How We Know Animals Think and Feel*, Crown Publishers, 2013. Virginia Morell, a long-time writer on nature topics offers a compelling look at animal cognition.

[2] Ted Andrews, *Animal-Speak: The Spiritual & Magical Powers of Creatures Great & Small.* Llewellyn Publications, 1993. This widely recommended book is a great place to begin the study of animal symbology.

[3] Francis Thompson wrote his long poem, *The Hound of Heaven*, in 1909.

Horses: Nobility and Resilience

Epigraph: From Kelly Wendorf, in a podcast titled "Flying Lead Change and our Evolutionary Kinship with Horses," an interview with Tami Simon on *Insights at the Edge*, at Sounds True.com. To learn about Kelly's work with equine-assisted learning experiences and leadership development, see the website for her organization EQUUS: equusinspired.com.

[1] *Habitat for Horses* is a non-profit organization in Alvin, Texas, committed to helping neglected, abused and homeless horses and donkeys. For those unable to adopt a horse, virtual adoptions are available. habitatforhorses.org

Cats: Creatures of My Heart

Epigraph: Ernest Hemingway, 1899-1961. The Ernest Hemingway Home & Museum in Key West is home to 40-50 polydactyl (six-toed) cats. hemingwayhome.com

Cats: The Wild Ones

Epigraph: Britannica. The "cat pattern" seems to have been established very early in mammalian evolution; early cats were already familiar in appearance before the ancestors of most other modern species were recognizable.

1. Robert A. Johnson, *Inner Work: Using Dreams & Active Imagination for Personal Growth*, Harper SanFrancisco, 1986. I highly recommend this wise classic for every dreamer. Do read Johnson's funny account of his resistance to his dream lion, p. 173-174. See *Appendix III* for more information about active imagination.

2. Bev Doolittle, an artist devoted to nature and native peoples, is known for her intriguing camouflage art. artifactsgallery.com

3. Lisa Rigge has published her article "When Bobcat Appeared" in *DreamTime Magazine*, a publication of the International Association for the Study of Dreams, Fall, 2019; and in *The Rose in the World*, Fall 2020, Issue 32.

4. Sarah D. Norton received her Ph.D. in depth psychology. The title of her dissertation: *Arctic Imaginings: Chasing Ice through C.G. Jung's Liber Novus into the 21st Century* (2019). Sarah is also Editor-in-Chief of *The Rose in the World*, a publication dedicated to "Inviting Wisdom into our lives and sacred spaces" and author/illustrator of a lovely little book, *Drawn to Dream: An Illustrated Guide to Basic Jungian Terminology*.

5. *The Red Book, Liber Novus* is an illuminated volume created by C. G. Jung between 1914-1930, covering his principal theories about the development of the personality.

Birds: On the Wing

Epigraph: Bible - Job 12:7.

1. Magic Questions, a tool developed by Robert J. Hoss and shared with the dream community. (See *Appendix III*.) You may access many free resources on Robert Hoss's website: dreamscience.org. I recommend downloading his "Dream Worksheet" which contains both his *Scripted Role-Play/Magic Questions* and his *Color Questionnaire*. His excellent book, *Dream Language*, 2nd Edition, is available there as a free download.

Snakes: Primitive Power

Epigraph: *John Muir*, 1838-1914, was known as the "Father of the National Parks." These words come from his essay "Yellowstone Park".

1. "Woman Sleeps with Python Every Night. Then He Stops Eating and Vets Learn His True Colors," by Ashley Brewer, October 31, 2017, Animal Channel.com.

Sea Creatures: Deep Calls to Deep

Epigraph: Psalm 104 praises God for all of God's creation and creatures.

1. *Dream Prayers: Dreamwork as a Spiritual Path*, 2002, by Tallulah Lyons. In this wonderful book, the author uses her own dreams to guide readers into increasing sensitivity to the spiritual realm. She is also the author of *Dreams and Guided Imagery: Gifts for Transforming Illness and Crisis*, Balboa Press, 2012.
2. *Night Fishing: A Woman's Dream Journal* by Katherine Metcalf Nelson, Gibbs Smith Publisher, 1997. Her dreams of the deep are richly rendered in both words and art – a great inspiration for dreamers wanting to bring their dreams forward into waking life.
3. *Free Willy*, a 1993 award-winning family film written by Keith A Walker. The story follows an orca named Willy, captured from his pod and sent to an amusement park where he is befriended by a young boy Jesse, who eventually helps to return Willy to his home.
4. *Women Who Run with the Wolves* by Clarissa Pinkola Estés, Ph.D., is a classic in the realm of the inner journey and an essential read for women and men intentional about personal growth.

Bugs: The Many-Legged

Epigraph: Donald Robert Perry "Don" Marquis, 1878-1937, authored the humorous 1927 poem, "Archy and Mehitabel," in which Archy, a cockroach, is unable to use the shift key on the typewriter for capitals and punctuation.

1. Richard J. Foster, from *Prayer: Finding the Heart's True Home*. The full quote is: "Our Adversary majors in three things: noise, hurry and crowds. If he can keep us engaged in 'muchness' and 'manyness,' he will rest satisfied.
2. The Enneagram is an ancient, robust typology of human personality types that I find enormously helpful. The nine types, represented by a geometric

figure, are taught by many teachers and schools. One respected place to begin: enneagraminstitute.com

Briefly the Enneagram numbers/types and their main characteristics:
    1: Perfectionist, Reformer
    2: Helper, Giver
    3: Achiever, Performer
    4: Individualist, Romantic
    5: Observer, Investigator
    6: Loyalist, Loyal Skeptic
    7: Enthusiast, Epicure
    8: Challenger, Protector
    9: Peacemaker, Mediator

[3] Amy Curran, a certified dreamworker trained by The Haden Institute, may be reached at innerdreamwork.com

Turtles: Ancient Ones

Epigraph: "Turtles all the way down" is a story with ancient roots, so widely known that its history appears in Britannica.

[1] *How the Turtle Got Its Shell* is a whimsical *Little Golden Book* of turtle myths by Justine Fontes and Ron Fontes, illustrated by Keiko Motoyama. penguinrandomhouse.com

Interlude: A Visitation

Epigraph: One of the countless maxims that have outlived any accurate attribution.

Part II: Focus on Themes

Epigraph: Robert Hoss, *Dream Language,* 2nd Edition, PDF Version, 2019, p. 214, edited.

Spiritual Menagerie

Epigraph: Cecil Frances Alexander (1818-1895), Irish hymnwriter and poet, wrote these words in 1848, based on the Genesis creation story. Her words constitute the refrain of the beloved hymn "All Things Bright and Beautiful" (# 147 in the United Methodist Hymnal). Martin Shaw set Alexander's words to music in 1915.

Diamonds in the Details

Epigraph: Robert Hoss, *Dream Language*, 2nd Edition, PDF Version, p. 142-143, edited.

[1] Peter Birkhäuser, a brilliant artist, began painting what he called "pictures of the imagination" after his acquaintance with Jung's ideas and the value of dreamwork. See the beautiful book *Light from the Darkness: The Paintings of Peter Birkhäuser*. One can also view his work on Google images.

[2] Robert Hoss's *Color Questionnaire*, based on color psychology, is available on his website and in his downloadable free PDF book, *Dream Language,* at dreamscience.org.

[3] *Numbers in Dreams*, by Doris Snyder, is a richly helpful tool for working with numbers in dreams and in waking life.

[4] Kerby Rosannes, a brilliantly creative illustrator, produces intricately detailed art featuring real and fantastical animals. I highly recommend animal dreamers take a look at his books and color books. Be prepared to smile! kerbyrosanes.com

[5] SoulCollage^R is a rich practice of creative expression created by Seena B. Frost and now widely taught and practiced as an intuitive process for self-discovery. Two websites to see: soulcollage.com and kaleidosoul.com

[6] Stephen T. Wilkerson, M.D., Ph.D., is the author of *A Most Mysterious Union: The Role of Alchemy in Goethe's Faust* (2019), which offers hope and optimism for the future involving the Divine Feminine.

Who's in Charge Here?

Epigraph: Robert Hoss, *Dream Language*, 2nd Edition, PDF Version, p. 135, 141, edited.

1   Myers-Briggs Type Indicator® (MBTI®) is a long-respected personality inventory based on the psychological types described by C.G. Jung and developed for wide use by Isabel Briggs Myers and Katharine Briggs. The MBTI testing instrument sorts for preferences – how one prefers to focus on the world (inner or outer), how one focuses on information (the information itself or adding interpretation and meaning), how one makes decisions (logic and consistency or people and circumstances) and how one deals with structure (getting things decided or staying open to new information and options). As an INTP, Steve Wilkerson is an Introvert who prefers Intuition, Thinking and Perceiving. A good starting point for MBTI: myersbriggs.org

2   Enneagram – see *Bugs* chapter note.

Composite Creatures

Epigraph: from Britannica. How might we apply what we know about the advantages of composite materials to our dreamwork with composite creatures?

1   Ruthie V., executive director and teacher at the Seattle Artist League, wrote this post on April 10, 2017, "Indian Composite Animal Paintings." Try Google to view these great images for yourself.

MoleCat's Revelation

Epigraph: Robert Hoss, *Dream Language*, 2nd Edition, PDF Version, p. 128, edited.

1   Robert Johnson, *Inner Work*, p. 189.

Life, Death and Resurrection

Epigraph: Robert Hoss, *Dream Language*, 2nd Edition, PDF Version, p. 130, edited.

1   *The Universal Christ*, Richard Rohr, Chapter 7, *Going Somewhere*. This book is sure to become a spiritual classic of our time.

[1] Joe Blake is a main character in *The Man in the High Castle*, a dystopian alternate history television series by Amazon Studies, in which the Axis powers won World War II.

[2] From *To Bless the Space Between Us: A Book of Blessings* by John O'Donohue, Irish teacher and poet in the Celtic spiritual tradition.

Transformations

Epigraph: Robert Hoss, *Dream Language*, 2nd Edition, PDF Version, p. 127, edited.

[1] *Calvin and Hobbes*, a highly acclaimed daily American comic strip (1985 – 1995) by Bill Watterson. The comic strips and books feature the adventures of precocious six-year-old Calvin and his tiger, Hobbes, who appears as an inanimate stuffed animal to others, but is a fully alive, philosophical companion for Calvin.

[2] Tallulah Lyons' frog dreams first appeared in her book, *Dream Prayers: Dreamwork as a Spiritual Path*. See *Sea Creatures* note 1.

[3] The Haden Institute offers two-year training programs for dream leaders and spiritual directors and hosts the Summer Dreams and Spirituality Conference. hadeninstitute.org

Ancestral Callings

Epigraph: Bible - Joel 2:28.

Community Connections

Epigraph: Excerpted from the book by Marc Bekoff, *The Emotional Lives of Animals,* New World Library, 2007, p. 30-31. Reprinted with permission from newworldlibrary.com. In this fine book, with a foreword by Jane Goodall, Bekoff goes beyond animal emotions to cover scientific skepticism and how we can ethically better care for our fellow creatures.

The Promise of More to Come

Epigraph: Luther Burbank, 1849-1926, was an American naturalist, horticulturist and pioneer in agricultural science who cared about the impact of our choices upon the generations to come.

[1] *The Photo Ark: One Man's Quest to Document the World's Animals* is a glorious book by *National Geographic*. A man on a mission, photographer Joel Sartore has been traveling the world for years to capture portraits of the great and small creatures living in zoos and wildlife sanctuaries, calling others to help protect the earth's biodiversity. He has taken 6,000-plus photos thus far and his valuable work has been featured in books, TV appearances and a PBS documentary.

[2] The amazing seafloor circles of the pufferfish, part of the male's courting ritual, can be viewed on many online sites. Especially see the *National Geographic* blog written by Mary Bates, August 15, 2013.

APPENDIX I
Glossary

Adapted from *Drawn to Dream: An Illustrated Guide to Basic Jungian Terminology* written and illustrated by Sarah D. Norton

Anima* – The anima (Latin for soul), as Carl Jung explained it, is the unconscious feminine nature in a man's personality. This archetype is personified in dreams in many different female forms, from seductress to spiritual guide. The anima can function as a mediator between the conscious and unconscious and also shows herself in the irrationalities of a man's feelings since she is influential in regulating behavior.

Animus* – Jung described the animus (Latin for spirit) as the unconscious archetype of masculinity in women. This personification of the masculine nature sometimes appears as a group of men. The animus can play the role of mediator with the unconscious and, as an influential regulator of behavior, it can be seen sometimes in the irrationalities of a woman's thinking.

> * While Jung himself saw anima and animus as gender specific, a more inclusive modern understanding is that everyone has access to representations of both archetypes, no matter one's gender identity or sexual orientation.

Archetype – Archetypes are universal symbols available to all, even though we may have no knowledge of them in waking life. Jung understood these primordial images, older than humankind, to belong to the collective unconscious and to represent contents in the psyche that were never conscious experiences for the individual. Archetypes include symbols found repeatedly in myths, fairy tales, religions, etc., including the hero, the villain, the wise old man/woman, the divine child, death, rebirth, transformation, to name only a few.

Collective Unconscious – The collective unconscious is the instinctive aspect of the psyche that retains and transmits the common psychological inheritance of humankind. A level deeper than the personal unconscious, it was recognized by Carl Jung as containing the totality of all archetypes.

Dreams – Manifestations of the unconscious, dreams speak in a language of symbols, images and ideas. Dreams can play a critical role in one's growth and journey to wholeness by revealing aspects of oneself that are not normally conscious. Dreams also reveal new thoughts and images that haven't before crossed the threshold of consciousness.

Individuation – Through the process of individuation, Jung believed, a person becomes a psychological individual – a separate, indivisible unity or whole, a single being embracing one's innermost uniqueness. Individuation entails becoming one's own Self.

Self – The Self, for Jung, was the central archetype, the totality of a personality, an archetype of order and wholeness. As the regulating center of the psyche, the Self is the highest goal of individuation. The Self often denotes the God within. It refers to a fully integrated psyche in which all opposing or conflicting elements are united. Symbols of Self include the quaternity (represented by sets of four or the number four) and/or a circle or a mandala (the circle squared, a symbol of wholeness).

Shadow – The dark side of the psyche, the shadow contains all the neglected qualities of one's personality, consisting of partly repressed, unlived traits that have been excluded from conscious experience. The shadow is made up of all that we fear, hate, and deny in ourselves, good and bad, whether these aspects of ourselves are consciously recognized or not. In dreams, the shadow generally (but not always) appears as the same gender as the dreamer, usually in a dark guise – clothes, complexion, etc.

Synchronicity – A synchronicity is a meaningful coincidence in which a dream or vision perceived inwardly seems to correspond to events in external reality. It may seem as though the dream has *come true* in an image, symbol, conversation, media reference or physical encounter of some kind.

APPENDIX II
Reading Recommendations

Getting to Know Your Animals

ALL GOD'S CREATURES
Daily Devotions for Animal Lovers (an annual publication of *Guideposts*)
Edward Grinnan, Editor-in-Chief

ANIMAL LIFE IN NATURE, MYTH AND DREAMS
Elizabeth Caspari with Ken Robbins

ANIMAL-SPEAK: The Spiritual & Magical Powers of Creatures Great & Small
Ted Andrews

ANIMAL WISE: How We Know Animals Think and Feel
Virginia Morell

BEYOND WORDS: What Animal Think and Feel
Carl Safina

THE EMOTIONAL LIVES OF ANIMALS
Marc Bekoff

HOW TO BE A GOOD CREATURE: A Memoir in Thirteen Animals
Sy Montgomery

THE PERSONAL TOTEM POLE PROCESS: Animal Imagery, the Chakras and Psychotherapy
Third Edition
Eligio Stephen Gallegos, Ph.D.

Going Deeper with the Jungians

ANIMAL GUIDES: In Life, Myth and Dreams
Neil Russack

DREAM ANIMALS
James Hillman

Online Resources

Dream Network, a respected journal published from 1982-2015, is now archived online for all to savor and read online or download in PDF. Visit dreamnetworkjournal.com. Seek Volume 25, issue 4 (October 2006): *Make Way for the Animals in our Dreams.*

The Rose in the World is an online publication, edited by Sarah Dungan Norton, "dedicated to illuminating and bringing the Wisdom of the unconscious, the spirit, psyche, and soul into everyday life." Since 2002 it has been supporting and connecting dreamers and dream groups through a rich variety of prose, poetry and imagery. To subscribe and download new and archived issues visit roseintheworld.org.

Visual Feasts of Dream Animal Art

The following two books are out of print, but both are well worth the effort of finding used copies.

LIGHT FROM THE DARKNESS
The Paintings of Peter Birkhäuser

NIGHT FISHING: A Woman's Dream Journal
Katherine Metcalf Nelson

A Few Dreamwork Basics

DREAM LANGUAGE: Handbook for Dreamwork
Robert J. Hoss, MS
2nd *Edition, PDF Version, a free download from www.dreamscience.org*

INNER WORK: Using Dreams & Active Imagination for Personal Growth
Robert A. Johnson

UNOPENED LETTERS FROM GOD: Using Biblical Dreams to Unlock Your Nightly Dreams
The Rev. Robert L. Haden, Jr.

THE WISDOM OF YOUR DREAMS: Using Dreams to Tap into Your Unconscious and Transform Your Life
Jeremy Taylor

APPENDIX III
Ways to Engage Our Dream Animals

Throughout this book, you've seen many approaches to working with dream material. Here I've compiled a few useful tools and practices for your convenience. As always with dreamwork, take what you can use and leave the rest.

Writing the Dream Report

- Date, title and waking life context
- How, when and where my animal appears
- Description of my animal(s)
    - Lifelike or imaginary – toy, artistic rendering, off-screen presence, etc.
    - Size, shape, color, number, sound, smell, tactile contact
- Intuitive *knowings* – my animal's age, gender, purpose, where it came from, etc.
- My animal's condition – healthy, ill, injured, free, confined, well-tended, neglected, etc.
- My animal's actions and demeanor – calm, threatening, frightened, etc.
- How I or others observe or interact with my animal
- Eye contact and its implications
- Words spoken and who speaks them
- Feelings I experience in the dream and upon awakening

Prompts for Processing:

- What are my waking life associations with this animal – in general or in particular?

- Do I sense this animal emerging from my personal unconscious or does it seem larger than life – an archetype from the deeper collective unconscious? (It may be both!)
- What synchronicities am I noticing in my waking life – sightings, references, images, etc. – and how do they reinforce the importance of this creature to me?
- Considering my animal's size, condition, actions and environment:
    - What part of my psyche might it be mirroring for me? (How am I like this creature?)
    - What in my life is it challenging or confirming or cautioning me about?
    - What question(s) is my animal asking of me?
    - What gift is my animal bringing to me?

Prompts for Processing a Composite Animal:

- What composite animal has appeared in my dream?
- What does this creature call itself? (the name I record in my journal)
- What are my associations with each of the combined animals? Consider each animal separately, noting all of the qualities you associate with each.
- What is its role/actions in my dream?
- How do I compare and contrast these distinct animal energies?
- What message might this creature, in its blended form, be offering to me?

Tasks to Continue Engagement

- Dialog with your animal, writing out the questions and responses.
- Bring your animal into greater focus through creative expression – drawing, painting, photography, collage, etc.

- Gather items that represent your animal – sculptures, ornaments, photographs, children's toys, books, etc.
- Reach beyond your own associations to delve into history, myth, fairy tales, religions, etc., to illuminate the archetypal possibilities of your animal.
- Consider embodying your animal through meditative movement – mimicking its creeping, stalking, flying, charging, hiding or other behavior.
- For a recurring dream animal visitor, note its varying manifestations and welcome it as your companion and guide, honoring it and your dream series as a vital commentary on your journey of individuation.

Magic Questions

Use the Magic Questions (the Gestalt-based, scripted role-play popularized by Robert Hoss) to become your dream animal (X). After reentering the dream in your imagination, respond quickly and briefly to these questions, without analysis, from the animal's perspective:

1. I am:
2. My purpose/function as X is:
3. What I like most about being X is:
4. What I dislike most about being X is:
5. What I fear most as X is:
6. What I desire most as X is:
7. What I most want to tell the dreamer is:

To learn more of Bob Hoss's dream processing methods, visit his website: dreamscience.org

Active Imagination

Active imagination, an excellent process for carrying a dream forward, can be especially helpful for nightmares – a way to confront and befriend your animal and imagine a new positive outcome. The following brief statements are adapted from Robert Johnson's *Inner Work: Using Dreams & Active Imagination for Personal Growth*, where he provides detailed and robust guidance for his four-step method, which I briefly mention here:

1. Invite the unconscious – encourage the creatures of the unconscious to come up to the surface and make contact with you.
2. Dialogue and experience – let your inner animal figures have a life of their own. Ask questions and be willing to listen or to follow.
3. Add the ethical element of values – the conscious ego, guided by a sense of ethics, must set limits to protect the process from becoming inhumane, destructive or extreme.
4. Make it concrete with physical ritual – incarnate your active imagination by connecting it in some way to your practical daily life.

Praying Your Dreams

My first spiritual director blessed me many years ago with a process she called *Praying Your Dreams*, illuminating a dream through the light of the holy. Here is what I learned from her:

1. In the left column, record all elements of the dream.
2. In the middle column, write conscious connections with one's current life.
3. In the right column, answer the question: What less conscious or unknown parts of me might the elements in column 1 represent?

4. Read over all you've written with the desire to notice the Holy Spirit's movement.
5. Complete the sentence: The message seems to be…
6. Remain with the mystery in centering prayer for 20 minutes.
7. After prayer, re-read all that you've written and add to or restate the message as the Spirit moves.

In memory of Sister Adeline O'Donoghue
Ruah Center, Villa de Matel Convent, Houston

APPENDIX IV
Guided Meditation with a Dream Animal

The following meditation may be used alone or with a dream group where each member chooses a personal dream animal to invite forward. In a group, one person would slowly read the meditation, allowing time to ponder and be with the experience.

To use the meditation alone, you may wish to record a personalized version in your own voice to play back as you listen and relax with closed eyes. You may customize the setting for your particular dream animal – its natural habitat, the actual dream setting or another place into which you wish to invite your creature and its energy.

Take a comfortable seat and spend a time in deep breathing.
Envision a peaceful place of your choosing – perhaps a simple grassy meadow.
Cross a threshold into this pleasant setting.
The weather is perfect – warm and sunny with a gentle breeze.
As you enter, you see your dream creature ahead in the center of the area.
Notice how it feels to see your animal watching and waiting for you.
Breathe.
You see a small bench near your animal where you may sit if you choose.
Gaze at your animal and let it gaze upon you.
Notice what feelings emerge during this eye contact.
If it seems right, stand up and gently close the space between you.
Notice who is moving – you, your animal or both of you.
Breathe.
Be with your experience of this movement.
When you are near your animal, enter a time of communication with or without words.

Invite your animal to express its nature, its purpose, its desires.
Receive any physical contact that may spontaneously occur.
Be with what happens and experience this communion.
Breathe.
Be present in the moment until the energy subsides.
Thank your creature in whatever way seems fitting.
Gently leave the meadow behind, knowing you can return there any time you wish.

After meditating, honor the experience through journaling, creative expression or ritual to bring it into your daily life. Consider inviting other dream animals to meet you in such an imagined space.

ACKNOWLEDGMENTS

To all the dear dreamers who responded to my call and joined me in these pages, my deepest gratitude. Among you are close friends and delightful new acquaintances, new dreamworkers and those who've been dream-tending for decades. As a group you've been admirably generous and vulnerable in sharing your deepest selves, offering your dream animals and experiences that I might weave them into this book of encouragement for others. Throughout the writing process, I've held each of your dreams in sacred trust and I'm indebted to you for your patience with my persistence as I revised (and revised!) and shaped your material for print. I would love to thank you each by name, however, to honor those who've chosen pseudonyms or anonymity, I must offer this general note of lasting appreciation to you all: *You are the best! I pray your dream rivers flow on, deep and clear and sparkling!*

I offer sincere thanks to family and friends who have stood by supportively as I wrote this book, inquiring about my progress and urging me forward. Others to whom I'm indebted are many, including Mike Luedde, my spiritual director, a longtime dreamworker and dream teacher for his willingness to hear my dreams and to provide often-surprising new ways of thinking about them. And I offer a special word of thanks to John August Swanson, the brilliant Biblical artist who graciously allowed me to use his *Peaceable Kingdom* for the cover of the book. The vibrant energy of his art inspires me and makes me smile, and I was additionally pleased to know that he, too, journals his dreams.

Thanks also to Stephanie Schottel and Mary Ann Matthys, my two diligent readers who reviewed every page of the manuscript with an eye to how other dreamers might receive this material. (I am solely responsible for all errors and awkward passages that linger or have crept in between their readings and publication.)

Finally, I wish to acknowledge my friends in the Bay Harbour Dream Group, the leadership and faculty of The Haden Institute, and all the Haden Summer Dream Conference participants who have been mentoring me with their wisdom for years. Thank you all!

Connie Bovier

ABOUT THE AUTHOR

Constance Bovier is a professional writer of fiction and non-fiction whose wordsmithing career intersects with her deep love for animals and her commitment to dreamwork in *Dream Animal Wisdom*. As a spiritual director, dream consultant and retreat leader, Connie dedicates her time and energy to encouraging the spiritual growth of others. She created and led annual *JourneyWomen* Retreats for her church for many years while serving as a board and faculty member for the *Charis Spiritual Director Training Program* of the United Methodist Church in Texas. In addition to facilitating dream groups and classes, she leads *Sacred Landscape of Dreams* workshops. She is the author of two inspirational books, *More God: From the Twelve Steps into Deeper Faith* and *From the Crucible: When Recovery and Religion Merge*; as well as a collection of short fiction, *Restoring Hope*. Connie shares life with her family and housecats and tends community cats as part of her service to God's creatures and creation.

She may be reached at cjbovier@icloud.com